Performance-Based Curriculum for Music and the Visual Arts

From Knowing to Showing

Helen L. Burz
Kit Marshall

Performance-Based Curriculum for Language Arts

Performance-Based Curriculum for Mathematics

Performance-Based Curriculum for Music
  and the Visual Arts

Performance-Based Curriculum for Science

Performance-Based Curriculum for Social Studies

Performance-Based Curriculum for Music and the Visual Arts

From Knowing to Showing

Helen L. Burz
Kit Marshall

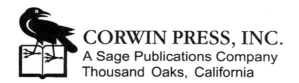

CORWIN PRESS, INC.
A Sage Publications Company
Thousand Oaks, California

For information address:

Corwin Press, Inc.
A Sage Publications Company
2455 Teller Road
Thousand Oaks, California 91320
E-mail: order@corwinpress.com

SAGE Publications Ltd.
6 Bonhill Street
London EC2A 4PU
United Kingdom

SAGE Publications India Pvt. Ltd.
M-32 Market
Greater Kailash I
New Delhi 110 048 India

Printed in the United States of America

Library of Congress Cataloging-in-Publication Data

Burz, Helen L.
    Performance-based curriculum for music and the visual arts: From knowing to showing /
Helen L. Burz, Kit Marshall.
        p. cm. — (From knowing to showing)
    Includes bibliographical references (pp. 125-127).
    ISBN 0-7619-7535-7 (cloth : acid-free paper) — ISBN 0-7619-7536-5 (pbk.: acid-free paper)
        1. Arts — Study and teaching. 2. Music — Instruction and study. 3. Competency-based
education. I. Marshall, Kit. II. Title. III. Series: Burz, Helen L. From knowing to showing.
    LB1591 .B84 1999
    700'.71— dc21

                                                                                                99-6280

This book is printed on acid-free paper.

99 00 01 02 03 04 05 10 9 8 7 6 5 4 3 2 1

Production Editor: S. Marlene Head
Typesetter: Birmingham Letter & Graphic Services
Cover Designer: Tracy E. Miller

TABLE OF CONTENTS

PREFACE

Traditionally, textbooks and curriculum guides have reflected a focus on content coverage. Districts, schools, and educational systems have looked to publishers to define, at least in general terms, *what* should be taught and the order in which it should be taught. The result has been to place an emphasis on what students need to *know*, often with little direction regarding the role of relevance and meaning for the learning.

The technological impact on society and a scan of future trends clearly delivers the message that just teaching information and "covering the book" is no longer a sufficient focus for instructional systems. Instead, instruction must go beyond the content taught and actively engage learners in demonstrating how they can select, interpret, use, and share selected information. Educators are quick to accept this shift but are faced with a real need for models that depict ways this might occur.

Performance-Based Curriculum for Music and the Visual Arts provides a unique model for taking instruction from the traditional focus on content to a student-centered focus that aligns selected content with quality and context.

Because of the focus on content related to a particular content discipline, textbooks and curriculum frameworks and guides have had a strong influence on *how* content is taught. The result, often, has been to teach facts and basic functional skills in isolation of a meaningful, learner-centered approach. There has been no purpose in mind beyond having students know certain information and skills. These previous frameworks and guides have also separated curriculum from instruction and assessment. *Performance-Based Curriculum for Music and the Visual Arts* offers a new organization and alignment of curriculum, instruction, and assessment around practical classroom application and does it in a way that readily allows teachers to use it.

Although not intended to be a complete daily curriculum guide, *Performance-Based Curriculum for Music and the Visual Arts* provides a planning framework that includes numerous examples of performance-based fine arts set in real-life contexts. The numerous performance benchmarks, at Grades 3, 5, 8, and 12, and strands can be used directly or as guides for customizing instruction toward relevant and meaningful application of important knowledge around critical fine arts concepts. *Performance-Based Curriculum for Music and the Visual Arts* can be used to guide the development of a fine arts curriculum throughout a family of schools or by individual teachers within one classroom or by an instructional team.

The framework is divided into four major sections:

1. Introduction to *Performance-Based Curriculum for Music and the Visual Arts*
2. The Content/Concept Standards for Music and the Visual Arts
   and Performance Benchmarks for 3rd, 5th, 8th, and 12th Grades
3. Technology Connections
4. Performance Designers

The Introduction is organized around a friendly question-and-answer format. This section is central to the remainder of the framework and provides the rationale and organizational structure for the book. The introduction also contains a discussion of performance-based learning actions.

The Content/Concept Standards for Music and the Visual Arts represent the best thinking of current national experts and provide the substance for each performance benchmark. These standards are organized by major strands within the discipline. Performance Benchmarks included in this section represent descriptions of what could be expected from a student who has a high degree of understanding of a content standard in a high-quality performance. For example, the student might be asked to solve a real-life problem or develop alternative solutions to an issue or question that requires a solid understanding of the content/concept standard at one of four developmental levels.

Technology Connections provide guidance for the application of technology in some manner to a performance benchmark. These strategies are appropriate for students who are accessing, producing, and disseminating information through technology.

The last section, Performance Designers, provides an analysis of the performance designer, which is a planning tool for teachers. It requires a focus on the key elements of content, competence, context, and quality criteria.

At the end of the book, design templates and reproducible masters (see Appendix: Blank Templates) provide practical tools that can be used to customize and create classroom instructional material that will empower teachers and students to be successful in "showing what they know."

ABOUT THE AUTHORS

HELEN L. BURZ

Helen L. Burz is a doctoral candidate at Oakland University in Rochester, Michigan, where she received her master of arts degree in teaching. She received her bachelor of science in education from Kent State University. Helen has taught at the preschool, elementary school, and college levels. She has also worked as a principal at the elementary and middle school levels. As an innovative leader in curriculum design and instructional delivery systems, she has led her schools to numerous state and national awards and recognition and was selected as Administrator of the Year in Michigan.

She has addressed integrated curriculum and interdisciplinary instruction for the Association for Supervision and Curriculum Development's (ASCD's) Professional Development Institute since 1985. Currently, she works as an educational consultant across North America, speaking and conducting training for future-focused, performance-based curriculum, instruction, and assessment.

KIT MARSHALL

Kit Marshall earned her PhD at Stanford University in educational leadership in 1983 and her master's and BA at Sacramento State University in 1968. After teaching across all levels, developing state and national dissemination grants in innovative educational design, and site-level administration, she pursued further studies in organizational development and technology. She has received numerous awards for her work in restructuring curriculum, instruction, and assessment. Her book, *Teachers Helping Teachers*, published in 1985, was the first practical handbook for educators on team building and mentor teaching.

Currently living in California, Marshall is an international speaker and trainer in future-focused, performance-based curriculum, instruction, and assessment. She is CEO of Action Learning Systems, an educational restructuring company dedicated to working partnerships with school districts and educational leaders.

INTRODUCTION

Authentic *performance-based education* asks students to take their learning far beyond knowledge and basic skills. A *performance orientation* teaches students to be accountable for knowing what they are learning and why it is important and asks them to apply their knowledge in an observable and measurable *learning performance.*

This shift "from knowing to showing" means that everything we do—instruction, curriculum, assessment, evaluation, and reporting—will ultimately be focused on and organized around these learning performances.

Educators, parents, business and industry leaders, and community members throughout North America are coming to agree that students should be demonstrating what they are learning in observable and meaningful ways. However, we have all been to school. Generally, our collective experience of what school *is* has been very different from what we believe schools need to *become.* If we are to succeed in the difficult shift from content coverage to performance-based education, we will need to have new strategies for defining and organizing what we do around *significant learning performances.*

Performance-Based Curriculum for Music and the Visual Arts has been developed to provide the tools and the structure for a logical, incremental transition to performance-based education. *Performance-Based Curriculum for Music and the Visual Arts* is not intended to be a comprehensive curriculum; it is a curriculum framework. The various components of the framework provide structure and a focus that rigorously organizes *content* around *standards* and *performance* around *learning actions.*

IMPORTANT QUESTIONS AND ANSWERS ABOUT *PERFORMANCE-BASED CURRICULUM FOR MUSIC AND THE VISUAL ARTS*

Content/Concept Standards

Where do the content/ concept standards come from for this framework?

This framework represents the best thinking of current national experts in the discipline of fine arts. Although there is no official national standard for content areas, the Consortium of National Arts Education Associations has demonstrated strong national leadership and influence that could form the instructional focus in a K–12 fine arts program. These recommendations have been used to form the content/concept foundation of this framework and are identified as content/concept standards.

How are the content/concept standards organized within this framework?

The discipline of the fine arts is organized by major strands within the discipline. These strands are listed and described in Chapter 1. They are Art—Structure and Function, Art in Society, Art in World Cultures, Analyzing Art, Critiquing Art, Creating Art, Philosophy of Art, Listening, Creating, Performing, Music in Relation to Art, and Music in Relation to History/World Cultures.

How do I know which content/ concept standards to focus on with MY students?

What students should know by the end of four levels, specified as Grades 3, 5, 8, and 12, is described at the beginning of each content strand section in Chapter 1. These levels are identified to highlight the specific developmental stages the learner moves through in school. A 1st-grade teacher should teach to the development of the concepts identified at Grade 3. A 6th-grade teacher should use the 5th-grade and 8th-grade content/concepts to guide instruction. A 9th-grade or 10th-grade teacher should use the 8th-grade contents as a guide and teach to the 12th-grade content/concepts.

These identified standards provide the content/concept focus for the performance benchmarks within the discipline and within the four developmental levels. Each major strand is identified by a set of content/concepts standards and is followed by four performance benchmark pages: one at each of the four levels—3rd, 5th, 8th, and 12th grade.

Performance Benchmarks

What is a performance benchmark?

In *Performance-Based Curriculum for Music and the Visual Arts*, a performance benchmark is a representative description of what could be expected from a student who has a high degree of understanding of a content standard and can use that content standard in a high-quality performance. For example, the student might be asked to solve a real-life problem or develop alternative solutions to an issue or question that requires a solid understanding of the content/concept standard. If the students don't have the knowledge, they will not do well in the benchmark.

Each performance benchmark is designed to target a particular developmental level identified as 3rd, 5th, 8th, and 12th grades. Many students will be able to perform at a higher level, and some will perform at a lower level at any given point. Where a student is in the bench-marking process will determine where he or she is in the continuous learning process so characteristic of performance-based education.

What are the components of a performance benchmark?

Each performance benchmark has

1. A **Key Organizing Question** that provides an initial focus for the performance benchmark and the content/concept standard addressed in the performance benchmark.

2. Performance-based **Key Competences (Learning Actions)** that specify what students need to do with what they know in the performance benchmark (refer to Figure 1.1, The Learning Actions Wheel, on page 6).

3. **Key Concepts and Content** from the discipline that define what students need to know in the performance benchmark.

4. **Two Performance Tasks**, or prompts, that provide the purpose, focus, and authenticity to the performance benchmarks. Having two tasks allows a teacher to ask for a group or individual performance, or even to ask for a repeat performance.

5. **Quality Criteria** or **"Look fors"** that precisely describe what a student would do to perform at a high-quality level on that performance benchmark. This component serves as the focus for the evaluation process. How well students can demonstrate what is described in the quality criteria informs the evaluator about continuous improvement planning goals for a student. The profile that results from an entire classroom's performance benchmark informs the teacher regarding next steps in the teaching-learning process.

How do I use the performance benchmarks to inform and guide ongoing instruction and assessment?

The performance benchmarks will

- Organize *what* you teach around a clear set of content/concept standards for a particular discipline

- Organize *how* you teach by focusing your planning on the learning actions that you will teach and assess directly during daily instruction

- Provide you with specific targets for your instruction—you will teach "toward" the performance benchmarks

- Focus your students on what they will need to demonstrate in a formal evaluation of their learning

- Communicate to parents that there is a clear and rigorous academic focus to authentic performance-based education

The performance benchmarks are primarily for evaluation of learning, *after* the learning has occurred. The performance designer, on the other hand, provides the focus for quality continuous improvement *during* the ongoing daily instructional process.

Technology Connections

How about a technology connection for **Performance-Based Curriculum for Music and the Visual Arts?**

A number of performance benchmarks in *Performance-Based Curriculum for Music and the Visual Arts* have a companion application that uses technology in some portion of the performance. If students are currently accessing, producing, and disseminating using technology, you will want to use or expand the strategies found in this section. These technology connections also serve as examples for teachers who are just moving toward the use of technology in their classrooms.

Computer Icon

If there is a computer icon on the performance benchmark page, you can refer to the companion page that will extend the performance benchmark to involve technology.

Performance Designers

What is a performance designer?

A performance designer is an organizer that is used to plan for ongoing performance-based instruction and assessment. The performance designer in *Performance-Based Curriculum for Music and the Visual Arts* uses the learning actions and connects them to content, context, and criteria. The power of these learning actions becomes apparent when students begin to recognize and improve their competence with each new learning performance.

How is the performance designer used?

The performance designer can be used to organize student performances in any discipline and with students at all developmental levels and in all grades.

The sample performance designers provided can be used just as they are or can serve as a starting point for new designs.

You are invited to copy the blank performance designers in the Appendix for your own classroom use, or you may want to create a new performance designer that fits your style of planning and thinking.

How can I design performances for my students?

Performances can be designed by following the steps provided in Chapter 3 on performance designers.

PERFORMANCE-BASED LEARNING ACTIONS

Learning actions organize what the students will *do* with what they *know* in each performance benchmark. Performance-based learning actions are based on four important beliefs:

1.	***Learning is a quality continuous improvement process.***	Students improve their performance with any learning when they have multiple opportunities to apply what they know in a variety of settings over time. As students become familiar with and adept at using certain key learning actions, the quality of each subsequent performance will improve. Students will be *learning how to learn.*
2.	***Certain learning actions, or competences, apply to the teaching/learning environment regardless of the age of the learner or the content being taught.***	The five performance-based learning actions coupled with continuous assessment and evaluation are applicable to all ages and in all content areas. The current level of competence with these learning actions will vary from student to student. There will be a considerable range of competence with these learning actions even within a single classroom or grade level. The focus of improvement is on comparison to a learner's last best effort, not comparison of students to one another and not on the content alone. Performance-based teaching and learning will focus on what students can *do* with what they *know.*
3.	***Successful people are able to apply certain key actions to every learning challenge. These actions have similar characteristics regardless of the challenge.***	When students learn, apply, and continuously improve in the learning actions, they are practicing for life after they leave school. Schools must allow students to practice for the challenge, choice, and responsibility for results that they will encounter after "life in school" is over. The more competent students are with a range of these learning actions, the more successful they will be in dealing with the diverse issues, problems, and opportunities that await them.
4.	***The problem with the future is that it is not what it used to be.***	Today's informational and technological challenges mean that schools must restructure themselves around a different set of assumptions about what students need to *know* and be able to *do.* Many educators and parents are reaching the conclusion that much of the information we ask students to remember and many of the skills we ask them to practice may no longer be appropriate or useful by the time they leave school. At this point, we ask the question, "If covering content is not enough anymore, what *should* schools be focusing on?" We believe the answer is "The learning actions."

THE PERFORMANCE-BASED LEARNING ACTIONS WHEEL

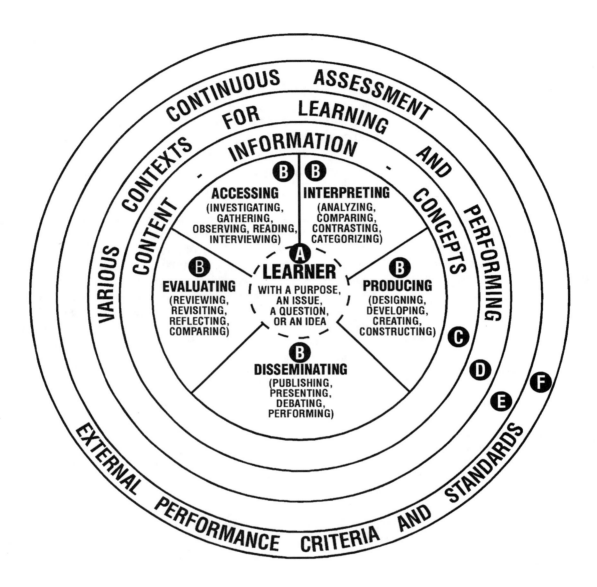

FIGURE 1.1 THE LEARNING ACTIONS WHEEL

Ⓐ The Learner

The learning actions are learner centered and brain based. At the center of the Wheel in Figure 1.1 is the learner with a stimulus for learning. That stimulus may be an issue, idea, or question that may have been suggested to the teacher by the content standards, or it may be something of particular interest to the learner. The learner is in the center because no matter how important we think the content is, it is inert until we add action to it. Everything "revolves" around the developmental levels, the motivation, and the engagement of the learner in the learning actions.

ⓑ The Five Major Learning Actions of a Performance

The learning actions include five major stages that learners will move through during any performance process. Let's look at the meaning and importance of each.

Accessing

What do I need to know?

How can I find out?

A performance begins with an issue, a problem, or interesting "lead." The learner accesses the information he or she needs to have in order to successfully perform. This information can come from a variety of experiences—but it must come from somewhere. Traditionally, information has come solely from the teacher or the next chapter in a textbook. In today's information-based environment, students must be adept, self-directed learners, determining what is needed and having a wide range of competences for accessing critical information and resources. Learners may investigate, gather, observe, read, and interview, to name a few actions. Whatever actions they engage in to find out what they need to know, *relevant* information must be accessed if the performance is to be as powerful as possible. Accessing is an important first step to a performance and a critical component of success as a learner in any role in or outside school.

Interpreting

What does all of this mean?

So what?

Critical reasoning, problem finding and solving, decision making, and other similar mental processes are what we must do as a part of any important learning that we intend to use in some way. Here, we must make sense of the information we have accessed and decide which information to keep, expand on, or ignore. This component of a performance asks us to analyze, compare, contrast, and categorize—to somehow meaningfully organize the information to represent what we think it all means. This component is critical to a performance process. It clearly determines the level of sophistication and competence with which we can deal with the amount of information constantly vying for our attention and time both in and outside a formal learning situation.

Producing

How can I show what I know?

What impact am I seeking?

Who is my audience?

The producing component of a performance is when we translate what we have learned into a useful representation of our learning. What gets produced represents a learner's competence with design, development, creation, and construction—something tangible that pulls the learning together in some form. This component is the acid test of a learner's competence as a quality producer, a critical role for working and living in the 21st century. In life after school, what we produce usually has a focus, an audience in mind. A powerful performance will always have a clear purpose in mind, a reason for the performance, and an impact that is desired as a result of the performance.

Disseminating

What is the best way to communicate what I have produced?

How can I have an impact on this audience?

How will I know that what I've produced has had an impact?

The fourth learning action of the performance process is disseminating. At this point, we are asking the learners to communicate what they have learned and produced to someone, either directly or indirectly. This is also where the value of an authentic context, someone to be an involved and interested audience, is so apparent. Only in school does there seem to be a lack of attention paid to such a critical motivation for learning and demonstrating. This is truly the point at which learners are dealing with the challenges of a performance setting. Students may publish, present, debate, or perform in a variety of fine and dramatic arts activities, to name a few possibilities. Service learning projects, community performances, and a variety of related school celebrations of learning are all ways for the learning to hold value that may not be inherently present in the simple existence of content standards.

Evaluating

How well did I do?

Where will I focus my plans for improvement?

The evaluation component represents the culmination of one performance and perhaps the launching of another performance cycle. It is the point at which a judgment is made and plans are developed for improvement next time. The quality criteria (in the performance benchmarks) for all the learning actions are the guides for these evaluations. The performance benchmarks in this framework represent the personal evaluation component of ongoing learning and performing on a day-to-day basis, or the self-efficacy of the learner.

ⓒ Content–Information–Concepts

The learning actions are applied to the content–information–concepts identified by the educational system as being essential. Addressing information that is organized around major concepts allows the learner to work with a much broader chunk of information. Thus, the learner is afforded the opportunity for making more connections and linkages and developing greater understanding.

In this text, the selected information has been aligned with the best thinking of current experts representing the Consortium of National Arts Education Associations. This consortium consists of American Alliance for Theatre and Education, Music Educators National Conference, National Art Education Association, and National Dance Association.

ⓓ Various Contexts for Learning and Performing

A context for learning refers to the setting in which the learning occurs, or the audience or recipient of the fruit of the learning or the situation—any of which create a reason, purpose, or focus for the learning.

Traditionally, the context for learning for students has been alone in a chair at a desk in a classroom. However, the context can be an art museum in the community. Students working in groups with artisans from the museum can be engaged in observing and analyzing an exhibit in order to conduct a tour for younger students and explain significant pieces in the exhibit.

ⓔ Continuous Assessment

The continuous assessment portion of the learning actions wheel represents the continuous improvement process that is imbedded throughout each of the other components. An authentic learning community will engage in a supportive improvement process that is less competitive than it is collaborative and cooperative. To *assess* originally meant to sit beside. During key points in each component of the performance process, students will reflect upon their own work and the work of others. The role of the teacher in this process is to ask questions that guide the student's self-assessment and provide specific feedback to the learner about what is being observed. The conditions we create for this reflective assessment on a daily basis will determine the ultimate success students will have with the performance benchmarks.

ⓕ External Performance Criteria and Standards

The outermost circle represents the system's standards and scoring or grading procedures and patterns.

Remember, there are four critical components of a performance. The learning actions represent an organizing tool for a performance. They describe the components of the performance process. The learning actions also represent quality work according to identified criteria. By themselves, the learning actions are of little use. You have to *know* something to *do* something with it. In *Performance-Based Curriculum for Music and the Visual Arts*, each performance benchmark combines all four components of a performance:

1) Content–information–concepts
2) Competence: learning actions performed by the learner
3) Contexts that create a reason and a focus for the performance
4) Criteria that define a quality performance

1
CONTENT/CONCEPT STANDARDS FOR THE FINE ARTS—ART

WHY ARE THE ARTS IMPORTANT?

The Arts are important to all of us because they provide understanding, reflect cultures, build self-confidence, foster lifelong learning, stimulate creatively, and are a major source of employment.

Throughout history, the Arts have been a humanizing force — a force which helps students become more sensitive to and understanding of human behavior, themselves, and the world in which they live. The Arts, with their focus on student-centered activities, help foster a more cooperative environment in the schools. Through dance, drama, music, and visual arts, students learn to understand themselves and their world. The Arts enable students to embrace the diverse cultural backgrounds that are part of our society by recognizing and celebrating the various contributions made by individual cultures.

Students feel better about themselves and have more confidence in social situations when they are involved in positive, challenging, and enjoyable Arts experiences. The Arts in education provide students with unique opportunities to express themselves. When they learn to play a musical instrument, sing a song, or create a dance or painting, students have a sense of accomplishment and a greater feeling of worth.

The Arts are expressions of students' thoughts and feelings. As they share their visions of what they want to create and explain personal choices in their decision-making process, they develop many of the basic communication skills that are needed for success in school and lifelong pursuits.

The knowledge gained with experience and study helps students to artistically interpret the works of art which they perform or observe. Through the various arts, students experiment with the elements of their craft and express their personal feelings.

Lastly, the Arts also offer a major source of employment. The possibilities include architect, musician, dancer, painter, potter, teacher, fashion designer, choreographer, composer, radio, television, and many, many more.

VISION

The Arts have been an inseparable part of the human journey from the very beginning. Since nomadic peoples first sang and since hunters painted their quarry on the walls of caves, the arts have described, defined, and deepened human experience. They have also served as a connection for each new generation to those who have gone before. Thus, we depend on the arts to carry us toward the fullness of our humanity. We value them for themselves, and we believe knowing and practicing them is fundamental to the healthy development of our children's minds and spirits. But more importantly, we know from experience that no one can claim to be truly educated who lacks basic knowledge and skills in the arts. If our civilization is to continue to be both dynamic and nurturing, its success will ultimately depend on how well we develop the capabilities of our children, not only to earn a living in a vastly complex world, but also to live a life rich in meaning.

PROGRAM GOALS

All students deserve access to the rich education and understanding that the Arts provide, regardless of their background, talents, or disabilities. In an increasingly technological environment overloaded with sensory data, the ability to perceive, interpret, understand, and evaluate such stimuli is critical. The Arts must help all students develop multiple capabilities for understanding and deciphering in an image- and symbol-laden world. A comprehensive arts program should provide every child the opportunity to acquire the knowledge, skills, and the beliefs and values needed for competent participation in the Arts as a citizen or a continuing student. Toward these ends, our goals must be to have students

- Communicate at a basic level in the art disciplines
- Define and solve artistic problems with insight, reason, and technical proficiency
- Develop and present basic analyses of works of art from structural, historical, and cultural perspectives
- Maintain an informed acquaintance with exemplary works of art and artists from a variety of cultures, historical periods, and disciplines
- Relate various types of art knowledge and skills within and across a variety of academic disciplines

CONTENT STRANDS FOR ART

The visual arts involve varied tools, techniques, and processes. It is the responsibility of practitioners to choose from among the array of possibilities offered by the visual arts to accomplish specific educational objectives in specific circumstances. The performance benchmarks presented in this text are designed to address selected strands and their related standards at each of four developmental levels. The content focus for the strands is

- Art—Structure and Function
- Art in Society
- Art in World Cultures
- Analyzing Art
- Critiquing Art
- Creating Art
- Philosophy of Art

CONTENT/CONCEPT STANDARDS—ART

The content presented in the performance benchmarks is not intended to be a complete, detailed list of all the information students should know but rather represents essential ideas, concepts, and categories of visual arts information and skills. Educators should consider these examples as a guide for their own selection process as they relate these concepts and suggestions to local- and state-identified curricula and expectations relative to these arts.

Each of the seven visual arts strands is identified, briefly described, and then presented in terms of what students should be able to know and do by the end of Grades 3, 5, 8, and 12. Each strand will be introduced by a listing of the content/concept standards considered critical to that strand at each of these four grade levels.

PERFORMANCE BENCHMARK FORMAT

The performance benchmarks are sample demonstrations designed with content, competence, context, and criteria that students should accomplish individually and collaboratively by the end of identified grade levels. For each of the seven strands, there will follow four performance benchmarks. There will be one benchmark for each of the following developmental levels: 3rd, 5th, 8th, and 12th grade. Because these benchmarks represent different developmental levels, they should serve as guides for all teachers from kindergarten through 12th grade. The performance benchmarks are designed to represent a description of what could be expected from a student in a high-quality performance who has a high degree of understanding of the specific content/concept standard and has consistently experienced the learning actions.

The following template, along with descriptions, is offered as an advance organizer for the performance benchmarks that follow in the next section.

PERFORMANCE BENCHMARK FORMAT

A. FINE ARTS STRAND AND STANDARD NUMBERS		G. TECHNOLOGY ICON
B. KEY ORGANIZING QUESTION:		
C. KEY COMPETENCES	D. KEY CONCEPTS AND CONTENT	E. PERFORMANCE TASKS
		PERFORMANCE TASK I:
		PERFORMANCE TASK II:
F. QUALITY CRITERIA: "LOOK FORS"		

A. Fine Arts Strand and Standard Numbers

This serves to identify the selected fine arts strand and the specific standard numbers chosen from the content/concept standards pages that precede each set of benchmarks.

B. Key Organizing Question

Each performance benchmark addresses specific content information and is organized around a key organizing question. This question serves as a focusing point for the teacher during the performance. The teacher and student can use these questions to focus attention on the key concept/content and competences required in the performance task.

C. Key Competences

The key competences represent the major learning actions of accessing, interpreting, producing, disseminating, and evaluating. These major learning actions are discussed in detail on the preceding pages.

The actions identified are what the student will *do* with the key concepts and content in this benchmark performance. Those do's or learning actions engage students in demonstrations of competence in technical and social processes. Teachers must teach students how to operationalize these learning actions.

D. Key Concepts and Content

The information contained in this section identifies the major concepts that embrace the essential content and knowledge base that was taught and is now addressed in this performance benchmark. These concepts correspond to the standard numbers in Section A above.

E. Performance Tasks

Each performance task requires students to apply the designated content using specific learning actions they have been taught. This is done in a context or situation related to the key question. The performance tasks can be done individually or collaboratively. In either case, it is still the teacher's responsibility to look for the presence or absence of the quality criteria in action.

There are two performance tasks identified on each performance benchmark page to offer teachers a choice or serve as a parallel task for students. Both tasks correspond to the identified quality criteria.

F. Quality Criteria: "Look fors"

The quality criteria represent key actions that students are expected to demonstrate during the performance task. The criteria also guide the teachers and serve as "look fors" during the performance task. In other words, the teacher observes the students for these specific criteria.

These criteria embody the key competences or learning actions that students should have been taught in preparation for this performance task. Students demonstrate the learning actions in connection to the key concepts.

The criteria serve as a process rubric that guides the design of both instruction and assessment. They also serve as a signpost for the learners.

The criteria are identified following a "do + what" formula, which makes it easy to "look for" them.

G. Technology Icon

The presence of a technology icon at the top of a performance benchmark page means there is a corresponding example in the Technology Connections section. These examples indicate how technologies can assist students in carrying out the key competences required in the performance task.

ART—STRUCTURE AND FUNCTION

Content/Concept Standards

The visual arts are extremely rich. They range from drawing, painting, sculpture, and design, to architecture, film, video, and folk arts. They involve a wide variety of tools, techniques, approaches, and habits for applying knowledge and skills in the visual arts to the world beyond school.

What students should know how to do by the end of Grade 3

Artists express ideas according to their own experiences. Artists use a variety of visual characteristics in order to convey purpose and ideas. These different features cause different responses within the viewer. Artists use structure and functions of art to communicate ideas. Students should be able to

1. Recognize specific visual characteristics of art used to convey ideas
2. Describe how different expressive features and organizational principles cause different responses

What students should know how to do by the end of Grade 5

Through the study of art, youngsters will be able to develop an appreciation of the artistic value of a variety of artists and demonstrate value through their own creations. Students should be able to

1. Generalize about the effects of visual structures and functions and reflect upon these effects in their own work
2. Employ organizational structures and analyze what makes them effective or not effective in the communication of ideas
3. Select and use the qualities of structures and functions of art to improve communication of their ideas

What students should know how to do by the end of Grade 8

Art reflects, records, and influences. Artists react to trends and events that occur within their environment. Often major influences can be observed in individual changes in style. Students should be able to

1. Identify artists' individual changes in styles, which may change over time
2. Distinguish the differences between artworks that are whimsical, analytical, factual, spiritual, or allegorical
3. Define and explain personal preferences in artists' work, recognizing the influence of personal beliefs, attitudes, and ideas
4. Form and defend judgments about the characteristics and structures to accomplish commercial, personal, communal, or other purposes of art

What students should know how to do by the end of Grade 12

Students understand the relationships among art forms and between their own work and that of others. They are able to relate understandings about the historical and cultural contexts of art situations in contemporary life. Students should be able to

1. Evaluate the effectiveness of artworks in terms of organizational structures and functions
2. Create artworks that use organizational principles and function to solve specific visual arts problems
3. Demonstrate principles and functions in artwork and defend personal evaluations of these perspectives

Fine Arts:
Grade 3

Performance
Benchmark

ART—STRUCTURE AND FUNCTION
CONTENT/CONCEPT STANDARD 1

KEY ORGANIZING QUESTION:

What are different forms of art?

KEY COMPETENCES	KEY CONCEPTS AND CONTENT	PERFORMANCE TASKS
Identify Create Display Explain	Visual characteristics of various art forms.	**PERFORMANCE TASK I:** You must set up a new exhibit. Students will break into four groups. Each group will identify a prescribed set of pictures as either a photograph, a painting, a drawing, or a sculpture. Each group will create a display board in the room according to a category, putting a sign on each category and labeling it accordingly. Under each picture, students should place another label explaining if the work is a portrait, landscape, or still life. The final display should be observed and critiqued by the students.

QUALITY CRITERIA:
"LOOK FORS"

- Identify photographs, paintings, drawings, and sculpture.
- Identify portrait landscapes and still lifes.
- Discuss distinguishing characteristics of the various categories with a partner.
- Create a display.
- Explain the distinguishing characteristics.
- Evaluate the final display.

PERFORMANCE TASK II:

Your job is to create a display you can use to teach second graders about visual characteristics of various art forms. Gather approximately eight different representations of at least three different art forms. (photographs, drawings, sculpture, etc.) Create labels for your various categories and arrange everything into a display for your second graders to view. Add additional name cards distinguishing the art as a portrait, landscape, and so forth. Use your display with second graders and explain the various visual characteristics represented in your collection of examples.

Fine Arts:
Grade 5

Performance
Benchmark

ART—STRUCTURE AND FUNCTION
CONTENT/CONCEPT STANDARD 1

KEY ORGANIZING QUESTION:

How can art evoke emotions?

KEY COMPETENCES	KEY CONCEPTS AND CONTENT	PERFORMANCE TASKS
Select Analyze Describe Justify	Effects of visual structures and functions.	**PERFORMANCE TASK I:** You are a writer for an art magazine and must review the art of new artists in your town (your choice of artist). In your article describe the art as a photo, drawing, painting, or sculpture, and whether it is a portrait, self-portrait, still life, landscape, or cityscape. Tell how you feel about the artwork. What visual structures or functions contribute to your reaction? What emotions do you experience? Write about the artist's future. Will he/she be successful or not? Give evidence for your decision.

QUALITY CRITERIA:
"LOOK FORS"

- Clearly identify your purpose.
- Compare characteristics of art by looking at portraits, still lifes, self-portraits, landscapes and cityscapes.
- Describe an emotion that is experienced by looking at a piece of art.
- Justify your decisions with specific evidence in the artwork.

PERFORMANCE TASK II:

You are given four pictures of artworks. Working with a friend, you will select two of them (a still life, portrait, etc.) and explain the emotion you believe the artist intended for the viewer. Switch roles and do the other two pictures. Provide evidence for your decisions.

Fine Arts: **Performance**
Grade 8   **Benchmark**

ART—STRUCTURE AND FUNCTION
CONTENT/CONCEPT STANDARDS 2, 3

KEY ORGANIZING QUESTION:

How do you respond to various artistic styles?

KEY COMPETENCES	KEY CONCEPTS AND CONTENT	PERFORMANCE TASKS
Select Describe Analyze Present	Art that is whimsical, analytical, factual, spiritual, or allegorical. Personal beliefs, attitudes, and ideas. Individual artists.	**PERFORMANCE TASK I:** You are an interior designer and have been asked by a restaurant to pick art-work for the various dining rooms. There are five rooms to be decorated and each one needs a different style of art. Select one work of art for each of the following: 　1. Whimsical 　2. Analytical 　3. Factual 　4. Spiritual 　5. Allegorical Label each one and write a few sentences about it. Explain why you like the art and why you chose it for one of the settings. Present your choices and explanations to your teammates.

QUALITY CRITERIA:
"LOOK FORS"

- State your purpose.
- Identify unique components of each category of art.
- Compare the various works of art by their features (or lack of).
- Relate your personal feelings toward the art.

PERFORMANCE TASK II:

You must plan a tour in a museum. Select five pieces of art by different artists that you will feature on your tour. Make sure that one is whimsical, one is analytical, and so forth. Identify two characteristics of the artist's work and how each piece of art makes you feel. Present each piece to the viewers in your group and explain your reaction.

Fine Arts:
Grade 12

Performance
Benchmark

ART—STRUCTURE AND FUNCTION
CONTENT/CONCEPT STANDARDS 1, 2, 3

KEY ORGANIZING QUESTION:

What are some relationships between your artwork and the work of others?

KEY COMPETENCES	KEY CONCEPTS AND CONTENT	PERFORMANCE TASKS
Identify Create Listen Compare Contrast Publish	Effectiveness of art in terms of organizational structures and functions.	**PERFORMANCE TASK I:** Identify a current event or issue that has special significance to you. Create an original piece of artwork that reflects your feelings about this issue. Consider how the structure and function incorporated into your piece helps convey your feelings. Display your completed work and ask others to respond to your piece of art. What message do they get from it? How does it make them feel? Select a famous piece of art that also represents a specific social issue for the artist. How would you compare and/or contrast your artwork with the famous piece you selected? Write a brief paper on the effectiveness of the two pieces of art to communicate with a viewer through structure and function. **PERFORMANCE TASK II:** Identify a special issue that attracts a lot of attention from the general public. Create an original piece of artwork that reflects your personal ideas about this issue. Consider how structure and function incorporated into your piece can help convey your position. Display your completed work and ask for feedback. What message do the viewers get from it? What emotion does it elicit? Select a piece of art that someone else in your class created. Compare and contrast your work with theirs. Write a brief paper on the effectiveness of the two pieces to communicate with a viewer through structure and function.

QUALITY CRITERIA:
"LOOK FORS"

- Identify an idea.
- Review possible directions or alternatives.
- Represent the idea using selected materials.
- Review responses from others.
- Compare/contrast your with another.
- Publish your conclusions.

ART IN SOCIETY

Content/Concept Standards

Art and artists play an important role in society and make a variety of contributions through careers in advertising, media, product design, architecture, landscape design, and many others. Fine artists can express thoughts and feelings about political and environmental issues or reflect current trends in music or technology. Artists react to a variety of trends and events in their environments. They appeal to a wide segment of society through cartoons, films, and posters. Other visual symbols and products such as trademarks, brand names, or color and shape coding are commonly used to communicate messages and ideas.

What students should know how to do by the end of Grade 3

Artists hold many roles in our society and meet many needs. Students should be able to

1. Identify the ways artists work in our society
2. Recognize the artistic contributions we encounter daily

What students should know how to do by the end of Grade 5

There are ways in which people are involved in the arts in their immediate community. Students should be able to

1. Identify specific uses of art in business, industry, architecture, advertising, film, and so on.
2. Recognize the variety of valuable contributions artists make to society in general

What students should know how to do by the end of Grade 8

There are differences and similarities between popular art forms and fine art forms. They appeal to different audiences for different reasons. The art of advertising plays a powerful role in today's society. Students should be able to

1. Explain the differences and similarities between pop art and fine art
2. Analyze the psychological appeal of advertising
3. Identify works of art displayed in their community
4. Contribute to works of art in their community
5. Recognize that the values of a society determine the status of its artists and artisans

What students should know how to do by the end of Grade 12

Art is a barometer of society. Its ills and accomplishments are reflected in both commercial art and fine art. We can tell what is important to a society/culture by looking at its art. Students should be able to

1. Recognize and explain how social trends influence our emotional reactions while observing works of art
2. Discuss and work through the issue of censorship in art
3. Discuss and work through the issue of propaganda in art

Fine Arts:
Grade 3

ART IN SOCIETY
CONTENT/CONCEPT STANDARDS 1, 2

KEY ORGANIZING QUESTION:

How is art used in ordinary products?

KEY COMPETENCES	KEY CONCEPTS AND CONTENT	PERFORMANCE TASKS
Select Analyze Present Explain	Ways artists work in our society. Arts contribution to everyday products.	**PERFORMANCE TASK I:** Look through magazines or papers and select an example of how an artist's work is used in everyday life. Analyze the type of art you find and define how it is used. Explain to a team of students how this artist makes a contribution to society and if this contribution is important. **PERFORMANCE TASK II:** Survey ordinary items around your home or school and select three different items or products that incorporate an artist's work in some way. Analyze the contribution of these products and determine if the work is important. Explain your ideas to a team of students as you share your three examples.

QUALITY CRITERIA:
"LOOK FORS"
• Explain your task.
• Use a variety of resources.
• Select your target items.
• Identify the key points of importance.
• Organize your ideas.
• Present your ideas clearly.

Fine Arts:
Grade 5

Performance
Benchmark

ART IN SOCIETY
CONTENT/CONCEPT STANDARDS 1, 2

KEY ORGANIZING QUESTION:

What is the artist's role in the community?

KEY COMPETENCES	KEY CONCEPTS AND CONTENT	PERFORMANCE TASKS

Review
 	
Analyze
 	
Design
 	
Create
 	
Explain
	Art is used in:
	  Business
	  Industry
	  Architecture
	  Commercial art
	  Advertising
	  TV
	  Film
		PERFORMANCE TASK I:
		You are an artist and have been asked to design an object, a label, cover or package. Review such items as a greeting card, lawnmower, postage stamp, soup can, laundry detergent container, book or CD cover to get an idea for your own design. Draw, then paint the design on illustration board and give the product a name or title. Explain to a learning partner how this piece of art can make a contribution to the community.

QUALITY CRITERIA:
"LOOK FORS"
• Establish your goal.
• Examine several sample products.
• Create a draft.
• Clearly convey message through your design.
• Explain artistic connection to community.

PERFORMANCE TASK II:
You are an artist and you must design a poster for a musical or dramatic event coming to the community. Review several poster samples, then draw and paint your poster on presentation board. Include the name of the event, date, time, and location of performance, and an illustration concerning some facet of the event or content of the performance. Display the poster in the hallway or library of your school. Explain to a learning partner how this can be considered as an artistic contribution to the community.

Fine Arts:
Grade 8

**Performance
Benchmark**

ART IN SOCIETY
CONTENT/CONCEPT STANDARDS 1, 2

KEY ORGANIZING QUESTION:

What is the difference between commercial art and fine art?

KEY COMPETENCES	KEY CONCEPTS AND CONTENT	PERFORMANCE TASKS
Identify Analyze Design Develop Present Justify	Differences between pop art and fine art. Psychological appeal of advertising.	**PERFORMANCE TASK I:** Working in teams, you must collect at least three pictures (in magazines, pictures files, or computer files) of fine art. Be sure to identify the title of the painting and the name and period of the artist. You must also collect three representations or examples of commercial art. Identify the product or company and the special colors or shapes used in each example to make it appealing. Analyze all of the examples collected to find similarities and differences in audience appeal. Design and develop a chart or visual representation that would convey your conclusions. Present your visual and explain your ideas to another team in your class. **PERFORMANCE TASK II:** You have been asked by an advertising firm to design and develop a poster for a client. However, this client wants her current-day product to be presented in the hands of a person in a drawing or painting done by an old master. Find a representation of a product of your choice. Review a file of paintings or drawings done by old masters. Analyze them for a match to the product you selected. Using whatever materials you need, design and create your poster for the client. Be prepared to present your poster to a group in your class representing an advertising firm. Be sure to include your rationale for audience appeal in the poster you have created.

QUALITY CRITERIA:
"LOOK FORS"

• Identify a purpose.
• Collect needed materials.
• Recognize key contributions from all parts.
• Create a detailed representation.
• Organize ideas according to purpose.
• Defend with thoughtful evidence.

Fine Arts:
Grade 12

ART IN SOCIETY
CONTENT/CONCEPT STANDARDS 1, 2, 3

KEY ORGANIZING QUESTION:

What is the role of censorship or propaganda in art?

KEY COMPETENCES	KEY CONCEPTS AND CONTENT	PERFORMANCE TASKS
Review Contrast Compare Discuss Draft Write	Current social trends exist that influence our perception of art. Censorship in art. Art as propaganda.	**PERFORMANCE TASK I:** Review your art portfolio (or the work of an artist of your choice) and select a piece of artwork that could be considered controversial. Identify the social issue it addresses and explain its importance in today's society. Discuss the kinds of emotions it evokes. Is this a piece of art with a strong message or propaganda? Explain the two and describe what elements of art have been used to deliver the message. Draft and write a position paper that clearly reflects your opinion on this issue.

PERFORMANCE TASK II:
You work in a museum and must review a new piece of modern art that is coming into the museum. It has been developed by a very controversial artist and addresses a current controversial topic (war, abortion, pollution, etc.). Discuss with a partner the possible reactions this artwork might evoke. Determine if it is art with a strong message or propaganda. Compare and contrast the two possibilities as they relate to this piece of art. Draft and write a review of this piece for a museum pamphlet. Be sure to address the importance of the issue, the emotions evoked, the idea of strong message or propaganda, and what elements of art the artist has employed to achieve this effect.

QUALITY CRITERIA:
"LOOK FORS"
- Clearly define your purpose.
- Identify your target.
- Organize according to purpose.
- Clearly state main ideas.
- Support with detailed information.
- Describe the current social trends or mores which influence reactions to this work.
- Organize layout.
- Present accurate information.

ART IN WORLD CULTURES

Content/Concept Standards

As students grow and learn, they develop skills of observation, and they learn to examine the objects and events of their lives. They also grow in their ability to describe, interpret, evaluate, and respond to work in the visual arts. This development occurs through examination of their own work and that of other people, times, and places. Study of historical and cultural contexts gives students insights into the role played by the visual arts in human achievement. Through examination of the visual arts within other cultures, students gain a deeper appreciation of their own values, the values of other people, and the connections of the visual arts to universal human needs, values, and beliefs. They understand that the art of a culture is influenced by aesthetic ideas as well as by social, political, economic, and other factors.

What students should know how to do by the end of Grade 3

There are a variety of images and artworks in all cultures of the world. The study of arts and crafts as art heritage enables us to understand the nature of man. Students should be able to

1. Use a cultural environment as a source of ideas and materials
2. Know that the visual arts have both a history and specific relationships to various cultures
3. Identify specific works of art as belonging to particular cultures, times, and places

What students should know how to do by the end of Grade 5

The visual arts have played a significant role in the development of cultures throughout the world. Valuable information can be obtained from cultural contexts. Students should be able to

1. Compare the characteristics of artworks in various eras and cultures
2. Describe and place a variety of art objects in historical and cultural contexts
3. Analyze, describe, and demonstrate how factors of time and place (such as climate, resources, ideas, and technology) influence visual characteristics that give meaning and value to artwork

What students should know how to do by the end of Grade 8

In most countries, past achievements have served as the derivative base for contemporary art forms. Students can analyze common characteristics to formulate interpretations of meaning. Students should be able to

1. Identify and explain factors that have influenced the production of artworks from a particular culture
2. Differentiate among a variety of historical and cultural contexts in terms of characteristics and purposes of works of art
3. Describe the function and explore the meaning of specific art objects within varied cultures, times, and places
4. Analyze relationships of works of art to one another in terms of history, aesthetics, and culture, justifying conclusions made in the analysis and using such conclusions to inform their own art making

What students should know how to do by the end of Grade 12

There have been major movements in art history such as Impressionism, Cubism, the Baroque period, and the Renaissance. Through these movements, students can examine the contributions of various nations. The contributions and cultures should be compared and contrasted by examining, discussing, and creating art indicative of different cultures. Students should be able to

1. Analyze and interpret artworks for relationships among form, context, purposes, and critical models, showing understanding of the work of critics, historians, and artists

2. Provide cultural examples of how people in various cultures have visually expressed their emotions

3. Identify and explain examples of art that express universal beliefs and aesthetic values

4. Explain contemporary art needs as reflections of diverse developments in a culture

**Fine Arts:
Grade 3**

ART IN WORLD CULTURES
CONTENT/CONCEPT STANDARDS 1, 3

KEY ORGANIZING QUESTION:

How do different cultures use repeated patterns or symbols in their art?

KEY COMPETENCES	KEY CONCEPTS AND CONTENT	PERFORMANCE TASKS
Investigate Identify Create Compare Contrast	Major cultures. Art/crafts: patterns, colors, and symbols used in art forms.	**PERFORMANCE TASK I:** You are an artist and you have been asked to design a royal mask that will represent a specific culture. You need to investigate art materials/resources from your selected culture to identify repeated symbols so you can be sure to use them in your mask. Then create your design. When you are done, meet with another artist to compare and contrast your mask designs. Be sure your mask is easily identified with your selected culture.

**QUALITY CRITERIA:
"LOOK FORS"**

- Restate your purpose.
- Gather necessary materials.
- Identify art symbols representing a specific culture.
- Create a product using the symbols.
- Compare and contrast your product and symbols with another product.
- Explain your choices.

PERFORMANCE TASK II:

You have been asked to exhibit a collage (12" x 14") for an international art show. The theme of the show is Cultural Patterns and Symbols. You must select a specific culture, investigate art materials and resources on that culture and then, using old magazines such as *National Geographic* or *Smithsonian,* plus other materials of your choice, create your collage. Present your finished product to another group and ask them to identify your selected culture and why you included the specific symbols you did. Compare and contrast your collage designs.

Fine Arts:
Grade 5

ART IN WORLD CULTURES
CONTENT/CONCEPT STANDARD 2

KEY ORGANIZING QUESTION:

What can we learn about a culture from its art?

KEY COMPETENCES	KEY CONCEPTS AND CONTENT	PERFORMANCE TASKS
Investigate Identify Analyze Transform Display Explain	Unique characteristics of artworks in various eras and cultures.	**PERFORMANCE TASK I:** You may select a major culture such as Greek, Roman, South American, Chinese, Russian, or American Indian. Investigate art resources related to the culture you have selected and identify depictions of people engaged in daily life/activities. Identify specific tools used by the people in this culture. Study one of the tools and then transform clay or papier-mâché into a copy of your selected tool. Display your created tool for your class and explain how it was used by the citizens in your selected culture and why it is unique.

QUALITY CRITERIA:
"LOOK FORS"

- State your objective.
- Gather necessary materials.
- Review depictions of daily life in your selected culture.
- Identify your personal focus.
- Create a product that communicates your selected culture and focus.
- Display your artwork.
- Explain your choice.

PERFORMANCE TASK II:

You are to investigate pictures/slides or videos of a major culture such as Greek, Roman, South American, Chinese, Russian, or American Indian to identify people engaged in daily activities. Select a major theme from your investigation and create a mural that depicts your impressions of the culture's daily activities. Your mural can be approximately 48" x 48". Use paint and brush to convey your information. Display your work for others to view and be prepared to explain how your mural represents the culture you have selected and the unique features of that culture that you have included.

Fine Arts:
Grade 8

Performance
Benchmark

ART IN WORLD CULTURES
CONTENT/CONCEPT STANDARDS 2, 3, 4

KEY ORGANIZING QUESTION:

What is the significance of past cultural contributions to society today?

KEY COMPETENCES	KEY CONCEPTS AND CONTENT	PERFORMANCE TASKS
Research Gather Analyze Design Develop Display Present	Influences of historical and cultural contexts in modern society.	**PERFORMANCE TASK I:** Various cultures have made significant contributions to society through their art world. You must research and gather information on major contributions from two different cultural contexts. Analyze your findings and then design and develop a museum display using replicas, photographs, pictures, and your own sketches and drawings depicting the contributions you have selected as major. Prepare a presentation that examines the importance of these contributions in today's society. Present your work to a group of your peers or invited guests.

QUALITY CRITERIA:
"LOOK FORS"

- Identify your purpose.
- Utilize a variety of resources.
- Organize your information.
- Select the most appropriate information for your purpose.
- Prioritize your gathered information.
- Sketch a practical layout for your display.
- Arrange all necessary materials creatively.
- Review display for meaning and appeal.
- Rehearse your explanation and presentation.

PERFORMANCE TASK II:
You are to prepare a photographic display on three to five useful objects from two different cultures. Research and gather the necessary information and analyze it to make your personal selections. Take the necessary photographs of museum pieces, artworks, magazine articles, or replicas. Select your best photographs and design and develop your display for students in the sixth grade. Prepare a presentation to accompany your display that examines the significance of these contributions in today's society.

Fine Arts:
Grade 12

ART IN WORLD CULTURES
CONTENT/CONCEPT STANDARDS 1, 2, 3

KEY ORGANIZING QUESTION:

How do artists communicate through their artwork?

KEY COMPETENCES	KEY CONCEPTS AND CONTENT	PERFORMANCE TASKS
Select Identify Analyze Prioritize Organize Design Create Present Defend Justify	Major movements in art history. Major artists within these movements. Communication through art.	**PERFORMANCE TASK I:** You have been selected to design and develop a display ("show") of art for the eighth-grade social studies class that centers around a specific human emotion. Select an emotion that you want to address through art, then begin your research. Identify the different artists from various periods and their works that convey the emotion you are addressing. Make your selections and create representations (photographs, pictures, sketches, drawings) of these works for your display. Then design and create a personal work of art that reflects your modern interpretation of this emotion. Be prepared to clearly articulate your reasons for the decisions and choices you made as you present to the eighth graders. **PERFORMANCE TASK II:** You are to develop a thematic timeline to be on display at the neighboring elementary school. Your theme should be depicted through artwork of various artists from various art periods. Select your theme, and proceed to gather the necessary information. Be sure to identify the artists and their work that addresses your theme throughout history up to current time. Make your selections and create the necessary representations of the artwork (photographs, pictures, sketches, drawings) you'll use in your thematic timeline. Create a visual plan for your timeline, then assemble and construct your final product. Prepare a verbal presentation on your timeline that explains your selections and justifies your choices.

QUALITY CRITERIA:
"LOOK FORS"

• Clearly identify theme and purpose.
• Identify important topics/objects.
• Select appropriate and significant examples.
• Organize in logical sequence for the viewer.
• Create a visual representation.
• Review and adjust for clarity and meaning.
• Complete with necessary and accurate details.
• Use standard conventions for audience.
• Clearly articulate decision-making process.

ANALYZING ART

Content/Concept Standards

Like other content areas, art has its own particular nomenclature. For centuries artists and craftsmen have used the formal elements and principles to distinguish an aesthetic form from a chaotic one. Other areas that are addressed when analyzing art are the content, ideas, or subjects expressed in the art. Identifying media and historical context are also part of the analyzing process.

What students should know how to do by the end of Grade 3

Students must learn vocabularies and concepts associated with various types of work in the visual arts. They must exhibit their competence at various levels in visual, oral, and written form. Students should be able to

1. Recognize that there are various purposes for creating works of visual art
2. Describe how people's experiences influence the development of specific artworks
3. Understand there are different responses to specific artworks
4. Identify objects represented in artworks
5. Identify and explain parts, forms, colors, lines, and textures in a work of art

What students should know how to do by the end of Grade 5

There are terms that can address the characteristics or traits intrinsic to works of art. Students learn that preferences of others may differ from their own. Students should be able to

1. Compare multiple purposes for creating works of art
2. Analyze contemporary and historic meanings in specific artworks through cultural and aesthetic inquiry
3. Describe and compare a variety of individual responses to their own artworks and to artworks from various eras and cultures
4. Identify and explain how and where the formal elements are used by an artist

What students should know how to do by the end of Grade 8

Students develop increasing abilities to pose insightful questions about contexts, processes, and criteria for evaluation. They use these questions to examine works in light of various analytical methods. They should know, use, and explain the effectiveness or noneffectiveness of certain media to communicate ideas. Students should be able to

1. Identify intentions of those creating artworks
2. Explore implications of various purposes
3. Justify their analyses of purposes in particular works
4. Recognize, explain, and compare different styles of various artists/periods

What students should know how to do by the end of Grade 12

Art is analyzed by using specific language that is learned through studying and creating art. Students should be able to

1. Express sophisticated ideas about visual relationships using precise terminology
2. Form and deliver analytical statements about the principles and elements in cultural, commercial, or fine art
3. Describe the meaning of artworks by analyzing how specific works are created and how they relate to historical and cultural contexts
4. Reflect analytically on various interpretations as a means for understanding and evaluating works of

**Fine Arts:
Grade 3**

ANALYZING ART
CONTENT/CONCEPT STANDARDS 3, 5

KEY ORGANIZING QUESTION:

How is a work of art organized?

KEY COMPETENCES	KEY CONCEPTS AND CONTENT	PERFORMANCE TASKS
Select Examine Clarify Teach Compare	Responding to specific artworks. Elements (line, color, texture). Principles (proportion, movement, repetition).	**PERFORMANCE TASK I:** You have three pictures of drawings and paintings. Select one of these pictures. Examine it carefully and identify the elements of line and color. Look at it again, and decide how the artist has used the principles of movement, proportion, or repetition. Use your picture to teach a learning buddy (fellow student) what you know about the picture. Let your buddy then teach you about another picture.

**QUALITY CRITERIA:
"LOOK FORS"**

- Clearly state your purpose.
- Identify a specific picture.
- Select the important points.
- Identify the needed details.
- Explain specific procedures to another clearly.
- Find likeness and differences and explain.

PERFORMANCE TASK II:

Select a picture of a drawing or a painting. Cover it with a clear acetate sheet. Carefully examine the picture and then using a colored marker clarify example areas in the picture that show how the artists used color or proportion or movement or repetition. Now remove your acetate sheet and replace it with another clear acetate sheet. Give the picture to a learning buddy and direct him to do the same thing. When he is done compare your two acetate sheets with the picture and discuss how they are alike and different. Teach your discoveries to another team of students.

Fine Arts:　　　　　　　　　　　　　　　　　　　　　　**Performance**
Grade 5　　　　　　　　　　　　　　　　　　　　　　　**Benchmark**

ANALYZING ART
CONTENT/CONCEPT STANDARDS 2, 3, 4

KEY ORGANIZING QUESTION:
How do you analyze art?

KEY COMPETENCES	KEY CONCEPTS AND CONTENT	PERFORMANCE TASKS
View Identify Analyze Compare Contrast Explain	Traits of art elements: color, line, texture. Principles: proportion, movement, repetition.	**PERFORMANCE TASK I:** You have been asked to be a guide for a group of second graders at the art institute. You will be responsible for explaining various pieces of art to them. In preparation for this experience, you are to view a series of slides from the art institute on the paintings you will view there. Observe each one with a partner and discuss the artistic elements and principles each artist used in their painting. When you are ready, present the slide show to another team of students in preparation for your conducted tour.

PERFORMANCE TASK II:
You are a member of a team of four who will compete against other teams in analyzing art. To get ready for the competition, your team must review slides of famous artworks and analyze each one. When you are ready, challenge your first team for a timed competition in analyzing the artwork.

QUALITY CRITERIA:
"LOOK FORS"
• Identify your purpose.
• Observe each artwork carefully.
• Identify your selected target.
• Select points that are similar in other artworks.
• Select points that are different in other artworks.
• Present information with specific, accurate detail.

**Fine Arts:
Grade 8**

**Performance
Benchmark**

ANALYZING ART
CONTENT/CONCEPT STANDARD 4

KEY ORGANIZING QUESTION:

How do you determine the time period, culture, and/or style of a work of art?

KEY COMPETENCES	KEY CONCEPTS AND CONTENT	PERFORMANCE TASKS
Observe	Each culture, movement, or era of art has a particular style by which it can be identified.	**PERFORMANCE TASK I:**
Catagorize		You are an art historian helping to analyze the artwork coming to the gallery where you work. You have just received a shipment of pictures of famous pieces of art representing various eras, cultures, or movements. You have to observe and categorize each one so it can be placed in the correct room in your gallery when it arrives. Identify and label each work with a card indicating the name of the era, culture, or movement and explain your choices to your group.
Classify	Examples:	
	Cave Art	
Defend	European Art	
	Greek Art	
	North American Art	
	Roman Art	
	American Indian Art	
	Renaissance Art	
	Middle Eastern Art	
	Impressionist Art	
	African Art	
	Cubist Art	
	Mexican Art	
	Surrealistic Art	
	Chinese Art	
	Op and Pop Art	
	Japanese Art	

**QUALITY CRITERIA:
"LOOK FORS"**

• Select characteristics by which to sort pieces of art.
• Observe for specific characteristics.
• Categorize by characteristics.
• Justify your choices.

PERFORMANCE TASK II:

You are an artist helping to organize pictures for a book on the history of art. Observe the pictures you are given. Identify key characteristics and then begin to sort and categorize them. Each chapter will represent a different culture, era, or movement. Determine the chapters you will have in this book. Label them and explain your divisions and selections to members of your team.

Fine Arts: **Performance**
Grade 12   **Benchmark**

ANALYZING ART
CONTENT/CONCEPT STANDARDS 1, 2

KEY ORGANIZING QUESTION:

How can the elements and principles of art extend into commercial art?

KEY COMPETENCES	KEY CONCEPTS AND CONTENT	PERFORMANCE TASKS
Observe Identify Relate Present Justify	Commercial art is art that is created for use in marketing, industry, or business. Includes architecture, photography, fashion, graphic design, industrial design, illustration, environmental planning, city planning, landscape design, film animating, special effects, and photojournalism.	**PERFORMANCE TASK I:** You are going to interview for a job in marketing. You have been asked to bring in your art portfolio. It contains a variety of pieces of your work ranging from acrylics and photography to landscape design and clay. How will you present and defend your work to this potential employer to enhance your chances of getting selected for the job in marketing?

QUALITY CRITERIA:
"LOOK FORS"

- Identify elements of art necessary for the job.
- Relate the identified elements to the portfolio examples.
- Justify with reliable evidence.

PERFORMANCE TASK II:

You have been interviewing possible candidates for a job with your company as a landscape designer. The person you believe to be the best choice has very little experience with landscape design, but has a powerful portfolio including many other types of design work. Using examples from the portfolio, how will you convince the other members of your team to hire this candidate?

CRITIQUING ART

Content/Concept Standards

In a critique, students will study the composition of artwork. They will investigate the makeup of the work: its arrangement, the process in which it was done, and its organization. The materials used to create the work will be looked at and evaluated according to artistic laws. Items for consideration might include

- Feelings that are expressed in art based on overall composition
- Artist's ability to successfully express intent
- Symbolism in art and how it conveys meaning to the viewer
- Visual and psychological perception and how it impacts a person
- The use of media, subject matter, and theme in relation to meaning of the work

What students should know how to do by the end of Grade 3

The subject matter, color choices, and arrangement that are chosen to create a work of art will give it meaning to the artist and the viewer. Students should be able to

1. Identify and discuss feelings expressed in a work of art

What students should know how to do by the end of Grade 5

The way that the elements and principles of art are used will create different responses in different people. Theme helps to create unity and tie it together visually. Students should be able to

1. Discuss the artist's use of media, subject matter, or theme when expressing intent
2. Explain how a work of art makes them feel
3. Identify symbols used in works of art

What students should know how to do by the end of Grade 8

The integration of visual, spatial, and temporal concepts with content will help to communicate intended meaning in art. The use of subjects, themes, and symbols aids in the demonstration of knowledge of contexts, values, and aesthetics, which put meaning into art. Students should be able to

1. Interpret use of symbols in works of art
2. Determine the presence of meaning in a work of art
3. Combine knowledge and skills to evaluate works of art
4. Compare and contrast the relationships of social and cultural influences on works of art
5. Consider the importance of works of art to history, society, and careers

What students should know how to do by the end of Grade 12

Artwork differs visually, spatially, temporally, and functionally. These characteristics can be related to history and culture. Use of subject matter, symbols, and ideas in art can help to sharpen thinking skills and solve problems in daily life. Students should be able to

1. Explain a work of art using detailed critical description and examples
2. Recognize fallacies and prejudices that people bring to a work of art
3. Present artistic merit of any artwork based on art rules, historical influences, and personal experience of works of art to history, society, and careers

Fine Arts:
Grade 3

CRITIQUING ART
CONTENT/CONCEPT STANDARD 1

KEY ORGANIZING QUESTION:

How do you read a painting?

KEY COMPETENCES	KEY CONCEPTS AND CONTENT	PERFORMANCE TASKS
Select Identify Analyze Describe Explain	The elements and principles that are used to critique a work of art. The observer forms a judgment based on prior knowledge and personal beliefs.	**PERFORMANCE TASK I:** You would like to buy a painting for your bedroom. With a friend, go "shopping" through a picture file, magazines, a CD-ROM, or a museum site on the Internet. Select a picture of a painting you would like to hang in your room. Explain to your friend why you chose that picture. Describe the objects you see in the picture that appeals to you. Tell why you like the colors, textures, or shapes. Explain how this painting makes you feel. **PERFORMANCE TASK II:** You are an artist who paints pictures of book covers. Your teacher will give you the title of a book and three pictures. Pick the best picture for the cover of the book. Explain to a learning partner why you think it is the best one: Describe what you see; tell about color, shapes, and texture; and explain how the picture makes you feel.

QUALITY CRITERIA:
"LOOK FORS"
• Identify your purpose.
• View the selected paintings.
• Clarify what you see in the painting.
• Select the key points/ideas.
• Identify how you feel inside when you look at the painting.
• Express your opinion to a partner.

Fine Arts:
Grade 5

CRITIQUING ART
CONTENT/CONCEPT STANDARDS 1, 2, 3

KEY ORGANIZING QUESTION:

How can themes and symbols be used to put more meaning into a piece of art?

KEY COMPETENCES	KEY CONCEPTS AND CONTENT	PERFORMANCE TASKS
Observe Identify Analyze Interpret Present	A theme in a piece of art helps to create unity and tie it all together visually. Symbols in art help to promote more critical thinking when evaluating art.	**PERFORMANCE TASK I:** Select two pieces of art from different periods of time. Look at them carefully. Identify any symbols used in each piece of art. Explain what those symbols may mean. Compare how the symbols are used in each work of art. Explain how they made you think about the art. Identify something the artist did to unify each artwork. When you are ready, present your findings to a friend. Does your friend agree with you?

QUALITY CRITERIA:
"LOOK FORS"

- Identify your purpose.
- Select significant symbols that convey meaning.
- Express specific accurate details about your observations.
- Relate your ideas to another piece of art.
- Distinguish the characteristics that create a feeling of unity.
- Present your ideas clearly.

PERFORMANCE TASK II:
Carefully view a portion of a selected movie or play as though you were a critic. Take notes during the viewing about the symbols used in the script. Explain what those symbols may mean. Compare how symbols are also used in a painting. Tell how the director or author created a sense of unity in the play or movie. Present your review to a group of your peers. Do they agree with you?

Fine Arts:
Grade 8

CRITIQUING ART
CONTENT/CONCEPT STANDARDS 2, 3

KEY ORGANIZING QUESTION:

How do the concepts of space and time influence the interpretation of art?

KEY COMPETENCES	KEY CONCEPTS AND CONTENT	PERFORMANCE TASKS
View Critique Write Publish	Elements and principles are used in a special way to create a response in the viewer. The space and time in which any artwork takes place influences our judgment of that work of art.	**PERFORMANCE TASK I:** You have been asked to chose a sculpture for outside the new mall that is opening in your area. You will view slides of three sculptures completed by Marshall Fredericks or some other artist. Using the four steps of critiquing art (describe, analyze, interpret, judge), write two paragraphs about the sculpture you select for the new mall. Be sure to explain how the sculpture makes you feel and what meaning it will have for the mall's customers. Publish your critique and share with your class.

QUALITY CRITERIA:
"LOOK FORS"

- Identify your purpose.
- Observe for unique use of visual, spatial, and temporal concepts.
- Note the specific details that catch your eye.
- Prioritize your ideas.
- State your main ideas in writing.
- Support with necessary details.
- Review and edit your work.
- Design appropriate layout for your published piece.

PERFORMANCE TASK II:
You are an art critic for *Newsweek* magazine. You are given a picture of a current work of art and must critique the work in your article. Write two paragraphs using these steps: describe, analyze, interpret, and judge. Explain how the art makes you feel and how it might affect others. Publish your review and present it to your classmates.

Fine Arts:
Grade 12

CRITIQUING ART
CONTENT/CONCEPT STANDARDS 1, 2, 3

KEY ORGANIZING QUESTION:

How do fallacies and prejudices influence our judgment of art?

KEY COMPETENCES	KEY CONCEPTS AND CONTENT	PERFORMANCE TASKS
Observe Describe Clarify Generate Discuss Conclude Defend	Previous training about cultures or types of people influences our judgment of the subject matter of art. Inaccurate assessments of people and cultures may cloud our judgment of art.	**PERFORMANCE TASK I:** The class will look at slides of two different cultural works of art from the 20th century. Each student will write two or three facts about the subject matter in each work and then write personal statements describing reactions to the art. In collaborative groups, students will classify the statements and determine what type of judgments are made. Discuss the difference between prejudice or fallacy and fact concerning cultures and the art. Generate a conclusion and defend it with another group. **PERFORMANCE TASK II:** You are a foreign exchange student and you travel to a country very different from where you live. The country has many customs that are unfamiliar to you. You must go to the school there and participate in regular classroom activities. Your host teacher plans a trip to the local museum and there you see typical art of the culture you are visiting. You are given a picture now (by your real teacher) of an artwork of that culture. In one column, write a description of things you observe about the art that are different from your home culture. In another column, write what you think about the artwork. In a separate paragraph, write a few sentences about what personal experiences and influences shaped your opinion of this artwork. In collaborative groups, classify your reactions and discuss what type of judgments are made. Discuss the difference between fallacy or prejudice and fact concerning cultures. Generate a conclusion and defend it with another group.

QUALITY CRITERIA:
"LOOK FORS"

• Clearly state your purpose.
• Observe art for unique cultural features.
• Note and identify specific details.
• Document personal reactions.
• Prioritize your ideas and discuss.
• Develop a consensus.
• Draw a conclusion and defend it.

CREATING ART

Content/Concept Standards

Using art materials, learning techniques, and developing skills are the most time-consuming steps in the art educating process, but they allow the student to learn by doing. There is no single solution for all students; therefore, each student must have many different experiences in order to develop and express his or her own personal vision. Experience allows students to realize their own creative potential and that of others. As they experience a variety of media and materials, they learn new language along with the elements and principles of art.

What students should know how to do by the end of Grade 3

Children experiment enthusiastically with art materials and investigate the ideas presented to them through visual arts instruction. Students should be able to

1. Know the difference between materials, techniques, and processes
2. Describe how different materials, techniques, and processes cause different responses
3. Use different media, techniques, and processes to communicate ideas, experience, and stories
4. Use a variety of art materials and tools in a safe and responsible manner
5. Use and mix colors (e.g., primary, secondary, warm/cool, dark/light, etc.)
6. Use spatial relationships (i.e., depth, foreground, middleground, background, overlapping)
7. Create patterns with line, shape, and texture

What students should know how to do by the end of Grade 5

The visual expressions of students become more individualistic and imaginative. The problem-solving activities inherent in art assist in helping them develop cognitive, affective, and psychomotor skills. Students should be able to

1. Select media, techniques, and processes
2. Enhance communication through their art experiences, choices, techniques, and ideas
3. Analyze what makes their choices effective in communicating ideas
4. Reflect on the effectiveness of their choices
5. Draw, design, paint, print, and create using mixed media, fibers, ceramics, sculpture, and computers
6. Develop ideas by viewing other artist's work, trends, or events in our society, in nature, or in man-made environments
7. Use positive and negative space
8. Create 3-D shapes, collages, weavings, stitchery, clay pots, and wood forms

What students should know how to do by the end of Grade 8

Ideas can be developed by creative processes such as brainstorming, thumbnail sketches, and creative problem-solving techniques. Current events and the environment can also serve as inspiration. Students begin to develop an aesthetic position on art from working with the interrelationship between the elements and principles of design. Students should be able to

1. Apply media, techniques, and processes with sufficient skill, confidence, and sensitivity that their intentions are carried out in their artworks
2. Apply the elements and principles of design in creative and unique ways to solve or resolve problems
3. Demonstrate how the communication of their ideas relates to the media, techniques, and processes they use

4. Manipulate media, format, and subject matter to convey varied personal interpretations

5. Explore the use of advance painting media

6. Create symmetrically/asymmetrically balanced compositions

7. Use concepts of composition (e.g., center of interest, point of view, movement, etc.)

8. Use glaze and other colorants of pottery

9. Make an armature for sculpture out of wood, wire, or paper

10. Work in jewelry/metal cutting, sawing, hammering, soldering, filing, drilling, and enameling

11. Create a multicolored print using registration

12. Consider cause and effect and explain it

What students should know how to do by the end of Grade 12

Studies continue to extend the students' knowledge base and experience. Experiences need to include a wide range of subject matter, symbols, meaningful images, and visual expressions. The created products should reflect personal feelings and emotions. Students should be able to

1. Communicate ideas regularly at a high level of effectiveness in at least one visual arts medium

2. Initiate, define, and solve challenging visual arts problems independently using intellectual skills such as analysis, synthesis, and evaluation

3. Frame work appropriately for display

4. Design displays for events in the school/community

5. Submit work in local and national competitions

6. Continue refinement in jewelry, photography, or ceramic processes

7. Continue refinement in drawing, painting, or sculpting processes

8. Continue refinement in printing or computer processes

9. Continue refinement of mixed-media processes

Fine Arts:
Grade 3

Performance
Benchmark

CREATING ART
CONTENT/CONCEPT STANDARDS 2, 3

KEY ORGANIZING QUESTION:

How does an artist use elements and principles of art to communicate meaning?

KEY COMPETENCES	KEY CONCEPTS AND CONTENT	PERFORMANCE TASKS
Observe Select Sketch Clarify Create Share	Composition, joining materials together, horizon line, perspective. Elements (line, shape, value, color, texture, and space). Principles of art (balance, rhythm, movement, emphasis, proportion, unity, variety, contrast, and repetition).	**PERFORMANCE TASK I:** You are going to create a display in your school lobby that will show visitors a different perspective of your student body. To get ready for this project, you must put yourself in a position to observe legs and feet. Notice how they appear, how they move, and their positions when moving. Select one pair that you think is unique, attractive, or special in some way. Sketch out your idea. Clarify your choices of colors, placement, and movement. Create your unique picture showing just the legs and shoes in action by your selected model. Share your finished product by putting it in the display.

QUALITY CRITERIA:
"LOOK FORS"
- Identify your purpose.
- Select an appropriate location for observing.
- Identify specific details.
- Record your impressions.
- Select important details.
- Develop the representation with clarity.
- Display for others to enjoy.

PERFORMANCE TASK II:
Take a walk around your school and observe hands. What do you see them doing? Where are they? Are they ever touching other hands? What are they touching? Are they decorated with jewelry? Select a special hand in action. Sketch out your idea. Clarify your choices of color, placement, and decoration. Create your unique hand and share it with others by placing it on a class mural that shows other "Hands in Action." Display your mural in the school media center.

Fine Arts: **Performance**
Grade 5   **Benchmark**

CREATING ART
CONTENT/CONCEPT STANDARDS 2, 3, 4

KEY ORGANIZING QUESTION:

How can you use principles of art to communicate concepts from science or social studies?

KEY COMPETENCES	KEY CONCEPTS AND CONTENT	PERFORMANCE TASKS
Investigate Prioritze Design Create Communicate	Elements and principles of art. Types of art: drawing and painting. Sequence in the creation of art.	**PERFORMANCE TASK I:** Think of yourself as an illustrator who has been commissioned to illustrate a specific concept or topic. Select a concept or topic from social studies or science and investigate it. Prioritize the key ideas you plan to include in your work. Then using pencils or paint, design and develop a travel poster on your topic. Use three to four elements and three to four principles of art in your design. Make your poster communicate a message about your topic to the people who view it. Display the poster in your science or social studies class.

QUALITY CRITERIA:
"LOOK FORS"

- Identify your purpose.
- Collect necessary information from reliable resources.
- Select most appropriate information for your purpose.
- Include specific, accurate details.
- Create a sketch of your ideas.
- Develop your final representation.
- Frame for display using appropriate materials.

PERFORMANCE TASK II:
You are to select a country or region you are learning about in social studies. Investigate the resources for the information you need to design a map of the region. Prioritize the key ideas you plan to include in your work. Use colored pencils or paint to show the characteristics of that region. Use three to four elements and three to four principles of art in your map. Mount your work and display it in your social studies class.

Fine Arts: **Performance**
Grade 8   **Benchmark**

CREATING ART
CONTENT/CONCEPT STANDARDS 1, 3, 4, 6

KEY ORGANIZING QUESTION:

How can current events or the environment be used as inspiration in the creation of art?

KEY COMPETENCES	KEY CONCEPTS AND CONTENT	PERFORMANCE TASKS
Research Discuss Determine Design Create Present	Art is created using elements and principles of art. Art can be created in reference to the environment or a social work.	**PERFORMANCE TASK I:** You have been selected to design and sculpt a piece of art for your community that addresses an environmental or social issue. Research your selected topic. Discuss the topic with several other people. What do they think about it? What important message do you want your work to convey? With this in mind, design your sculpture. Determine the size you will create and select the materials you will use in this work. Present your finished product to an invitational audience and encourage them to share their personal responses to your work.

PERFORMANCE TASK II:
You have been selected to design a large mobile for a public building in your community. It should address an environmental or social issue that involves many of the citizens. Research your selected topic. Discuss it with several people. What do you think about it? Determine what important message you want to convey in this piece. Design your mobile. Determine the size you will create and select the materials and tools you will use. Present your completed mobile to a selected group of faculty and friends. Encourage them to share their reactions to the message you have attempted to convey.

QUALITY CRITERIA:
"LOOK FORS"

• Identify a social or environmental topic for your subject.
• Select the best references for your subject.
• Choose and apply your materials using quality processes.
• Decide the best means for displaying your piece.

Fine Arts:
Grade 12

CREATING ART
CONTENT/CONCEPT STANDARDS 3, 4, 5

KEY ORGANIZING QUESTION:

How do artists share their artworks?

KEY COMPETENCES	KEY CONCEPTS AND CONTENT	PERFORMANCE TASKS
Review Select Plan Create Display Discuss	Designing displays of selected works of art. Communicating with an audience through art.	**PERFORMANCE TASK I:** As a graduating senior, review your portfolio and select artworks in one medium that communicate a variety of ideas and reflect a high level of effectiveness. Prepare them for an open exhibition for the community. Display your artwork and be prepared to discuss it with interested viewers. **PERFORMANCE TASK II:** You have been invited to present your artwork at the community art show. Review your portfolio and select artworks in one medium that communicate a variety of ideas and reflect a high level of effectiveness. Prepare them for the art show. Create your display and be prepared to discuss it with casual viewers and potential customers.

QUALITY CRITERIA:
"LOOK FORS"

• Establish a clear focus.
• Identify possibilities.
• Create additional artworks if desired.
• Design your display.
• Form the basic structure.
• Develop the visual arrangement.
• Use concise language to present relevant information.

PHILOSOPHY OF ART

Content/Concept Standards

Art is a representation of reality. The artist chooses to portray life according to personal views of life and individual style. It is important to define art and discuss it in clear terms that everyone can understand. Students in art are encouraged to learn and use a specific vocabulary with which to discuss works of art. This helps them clarify their perceptions and develop aesthetic values.

- A philosophical approach enables discussions of the nature, meaning, and value of art
- It explores the emotional reactions evoked by art as well as the importance of art to society, careers, and history
- Humans are unique as the only living beings that respond to art

What students should know how to do by the end of Grade 3

Aesthetics is a branch of philosophy which deals with questions about the nature, meaning, and value of art. Students should be able to

1. Explain how the concept of beauty differs from person to person
2. Discuss how and why concepts of beauty may differ from culture to culture
3. Develop curiosity and interest in various art forms

What students should know how to do by the end of Grade 5

The meaning of art will be discussed using terms to define it. Students should be able to

1. Make discernments of sensory qualities (e.g., variations in patterns, surface, color, etc.)
2. Speculate about different forms of art and how people respond to them
3. Become more open to and aware of sensory qualities in works of art or natural events

What students should know how to do by the end of Grade 8

Our aesthetic response is conditioned by prior developmental experiences and by environment. Aesthetics allows us to articulate why art is valued for its own sake rather than as a means to other ends. Students should be able to

1. Critically reflect on experience and its relationship to the evaluation of art
2. Analyze the parts in a work of art for a better perception of the whole
3. Describe events and objects holistically
4. Communicate using appropriate vocabulary for responding to the aesthetic qualities of a work of art

What students should know how to do by the end of Grade 12

Aesthetics can answer the questions: "What is art?" and "What does art offer that is different from what other objects can offer?" Aesthetics can also answer, "What is the unique nature of the experience that can result from looking at art?" Students should be able to

1. Classify, sequence, compare, and contrast aesthetic qualities
2. Distinguish descriptive words from evaluative words
3. Distinguish opinions from logical arguments, and objective statements from subjective statements
4. Discuss and consider the relationship of the values of the culture with the values of the artist and the individual
5. Discuss assumptions and their effect on literal and visual phenomena
6. Discuss the presence of possibilities and options
7. Discuss differences in viewpoints and reflective disagreement
8. Explain the basis or experiential reasons for their own attitudes and beliefs

PHILOSOPHY OF ART
CONTENT/CONCEPT STANDARDS 1, 3

KEY ORGANIZING QUESTION:
How does art make us feel?

KEY COMPETENCES	KEY CONCEPTS AND CONTENT	PERFORMANCE TASKS
Review Select Compare Discuss Explain Write	The nature, meaning, and value of art can be defined. Art is a representation of reality done in the personal style of the artist.	**PERFORMANCE TASK I:** You must review and select five pieces of your classmates' artwork to put up in the preschool for the students and parents to view. Pick out the pieces you think will make the students feel happy about being in school. Compare your selections with the selections of a learning buddy. Explain to each other the reasons you selected your pieces. After your discussion, write a letter to the preschool teacher explaining why you think these drawings will make the children and parents feel happy.

**QUALITY CRITERIA:
"LOOK FORS"**
• Clearly state your purpose.
• Survey all of the contributions.
• Choose your pictures.
• Describe the important details.
• Organize your information.
• Draft a letter, edit, and rewrite.

PERFORMANCE TASK II:
As an artist, a dentist asks you to select three pictures that will help his patients relax while they are in his office. Review the drawings of your classmates and select the pictures you think will help the patients relax. Compare your selections with the selections of a learning buddy. Explain to each other the reasons you made your selections. After your discussion, write a letter to the dentist and explain why these pictures will help his patients relax.

Fine Arts:
Grade 5

PHILOSOPHY OF ART
CONTENT/CONCEPT STANDARDS 1, 2, 3

KEY ORGANIZING QUESTION:

How do certain types of art make us feel?

KEY COMPETENCES	KEY CONCEPTS AND CONTENT	PERFORMANCE TASKS
View Analyze Explain Conclude	Identify styles of art. Express feelings about styles of art.	**PERFORMANCE TASK I:** You are going to serve as a guide in an art museum. Your job will be to take third-grade students through the displays of modern art and ancient art. In preparation for your task you must carefully view examples of work from these two periods so you can explain why people might get different feelings when they view these two exhibits. Carefully identify your own reactions and responses to the examples you have viewed and explain why you might have reached these conclusions. Then explain how a guide should get viewers to reach their own conclusions.

QUALITY CRITERIA:
"LOOK FORS"

- Clearly state your purpose.
- Note and observe details.
- Identify the different features.
- Select the most appropriate information for your purpose.
- Present your ideas with details.
- Express your final position.

PERFORMANCE TASK II:

(Note to teacher: Use slides if actual art pieces aren't available.)

You are on the jury panel for a big art show with three other students. You have before you a number of pieces of art. You see one that's from an ancient culture. You must explain to the other judges what you think about the artwork. Explain the colors, patterns, and materials that you see and also explain how they make you feel. Express your conclusions to the other judges about this ancient piece of art being in a show of modern art.

Fine Arts:
Grade 8

PHILOSOPHY OF ART
CONTENT/CONCEPT STANDARDS 1, 2, 3, 4

KEY ORGANIZING QUESTION:

What is the nature and meaning of art?

KEY COMPETENCES	KEY CONCEPTS AND CONTENT	PERFORMANCE TASKS
Reflect Design Develop Present Defend	Differences between major styles of art. Historical meaning of major styles of art.	**PERFORMANCE TASK I:** You are hired to be the artist for a sculpture to be featured in the lobby of a new hotel on Capitol Hill in Washington, D.C. Reflect on the importance of the task. What are the implications? Develop a paper-and-pencil sketch of your sculpture. Describe its dimensions and its material. Be prepared to defend your sculpture by explaining — Why it is art — Why it is beautiful — Why this particular piece would be good for the hotel lobby

QUALITY CRITERIA:
"LOOK FORS"

- Identify your purpose.
- Identify the important aspects related to this project.
- Select the areas you consider most important.
- Create your representations.
- Include necessary important details.
- Review and refine as needed.
- Provide reasons for your decisions and your final design.

PERFORMANCE TASK II:
The city council would like you to submit a design for a sculpture that will be the centerpiece of a new fountain in the park by the library and the city hall. Take time and reflect on the importance of this project for the community. Develop a paper-and-pencil sketch of your proposed sculpture. Provide the dimensions and the materials you will use. Be prepared to defend your work by explaining

— Why it is art
— Why it is beautiful
— Why it would be perfect for the city park

Fine Arts:
Grade 12

PHILOSOPHY OF ART
CONTENT/CONCEPT STANDARDS 1, 2, 3, 4

KEY ORGANIZING QUESTION:

How does aesthetics help us discover how we feel about art and verbalize our thoughts?

KEY COMPETENCES	KEY CONCEPTS AND CONTENT	PERFORMANCE TASKS
Investigate Listen Design Develop Explain Defend	Nature and meaning of art. Cultural factors that changed art. Social factors that changed art.	**PERFORMANCE TASK I:** You are an art director and must design artwork for the cover of a concert program. Listen to the recorded works of the planned concert program and then design the best cover for the program. Develop a defense for your design and present it along with your completed design to a panel of your peers. Use objective and evaluative statements in your defense.

QUALITY CRITERIA:
"LOOK FORS"

• Clarify your purpose and mission.
• Collect necessary information.
• Organize according to your purpose.
• Create a representation of your ideas.
• Include necessary details.
• Review and make adjustments as necessary.
• Develop the final product.
• Use objective reasoning when describing and presenting art.
• Verbally justify reasons for your decisions.

PERFORMANCE TASK II:
You are an artist hired by a rock band to design a cover for their new CD. Listen to the content of the disc and design the cover. Explain why your design expresses what the group is all about. Explain by talking about the individual items used in your design. You should also explain your choice of colors, patterns, and shapes that contribute to the artwork as a whole. Defend your design to a panel of your peers by explaining why your cover will help sell the CD.

2
CONTENT/CONCEPT STANDARDS FOR THE FINE ARTS–MUSIC

WHY IS MUSIC IMPORTANT?

Music is deeply embedded in our everyday lives. Music speaks to our emotions, imaginations, and intellect. Music gives us a glimpse of what people have felt, thought, and valued over the ages, and provides us with a picture of our own expressed ideas and feelings. Music shows us that people of diverse races and cultures have unique ways of expressing themselves, yet share similar interests, concerns, and ways of seeing things. The study of music can help students develop a sense of connection with the past and with people of various races and cultures, and an understanding of human achievement.

Through the study of music, students encounter problems that require them to come up with solutions and to make decisions. In so doing, students develop creative and critical-thinking skills, and experience a sense of fulfillment and achievement.

Music is a form of communication and a means of expression. Students who study music and master its skills develop the ability to explore and express their ideas in a medium that can be more powerful than words or pictures.

Music is a way of thinking and knowing about the world in which we live. For many students, music is the major route to learning, their most developed intelligence, and their way of identifying foundation skills. Music is a way to apply mathematical and logical reasoning skills, explore ideas, and have the satisfaction of making abstract ideas concrete.

As a universal language, music allows us to express our common aspirations and to respond to the expressions of others in deep and significant ways.

VISION

The music program should be designed to prepare each student to become an informed citizen through experiences in a variety of musical forms, styles, and genres. The music program should address a two-fold purpose. First, the design should allow every student to

- Express their personal thoughts and feelings through creating and performing music
- Respond to works of music by identifying and explaining the important features found in the music
- Demonstrate an understanding that music expresses itself deeply to humans in a language that cannot be paraphrased in words

Second, the program should provide opportunities for students to identify their own exceptional abilities in music and to develop their personal skills in performing, listening, and creating.

PROGRAM GOALS

The development of music literacy for every student will be achieved through study in the following four broad topics:

- Understanding Form in Music
- Exploring Meaning in Music
- Understanding the Function of Music
- Experiencing the Creative Process in Music

Students will identify, describe, and manipulate patterns that are used to create music.

Students will demonstrate how music stimulates self-awareness, both emotionally and intellectually.

Students will be receptive to the music ideas of others and will demonstrate an understanding of how music reflects cultural and historical differences.

Students will identify, describe, and critique the use of a variety of components of music through directed, purposeful listening.

Students will express themselves through interpreting music symbols and applying learned skills in performance.

PROCESS SKILLS

Creating, performing, and responding to music are the fundamental music processes in which humans engage. Students learn by doing music in an authentic context, with expert guidance and many forms of feedback. The role of the teacher in the music development of the child cannot be underestimated, for many students of music learn best when artistic and skilled music making is modeled for them.

Students create music, demonstrating their knowledge of the materials or elements of music, their concepts of form or structure, and their ability to express ideas or feelings through the medium of music.

Students perform or present music aurally, demonstrating their skills in playing or singing, and in interpreting symbols of the language of music.

Students respond to music through informed listening, demonstrating their skills in critiquing and analyzing. Students also respond to music with the entire realm of human feeling and expression, both privately, and with others.

Students learn music skills sequentially. Skills are best developed when they are practiced in a variety of contexts, which are systematically and thoughtfully designed.

CONTENT STRANDS FOR MUSIC

The performance benchmarks presented in this text are designed to address each of these strands and their related standards at each of four levels. These five strands are

- Listening
- Creating
- Performing
- Music in Relation to Art
- Music in Relation to History/World Cultures

These five strands and the standards that accompany them are designed to address the overall curriculum design and comprehensive student performance expectations of a music program of excellence.

CONTENT/CONCEPT STANDARDS—MUSIC

The content presented in the performance benchmarks is not intended to be a complete, detailed list of all the information students should know but rather represents essential ideas, concepts, and categories of music information and skills. Educators should consider these examples as a guide for their own selection process as they relate these concepts and suggestions to local- and state-identified curricula and expectations relative to these arts.

Each of the seven visual arts strands is identified, briefly described, and then presented in terms of what students should be able to know and do by the end of Grades 3, 5, 8, and 12. Each strand will be introduced by a listing of the content/concept standards considered critical to that strand at each of these four grade levels.

PERFORMANCE BENCHMARK FORMAT

The performance benchmarks are sample demonstrations designed with content, competence, context, and criteria that students should accomplish individually and collaboratively by the end of identified grade levels. For each of the seven strands, there will follow four performance benchmarks. There will be one benchmark for each of the following developmental levels: 3rd, 5th, 8th, and 12th grade. Because these benchmarks represent different developmental levels, they should serve as guides for all teachers from kindergarten through 12th grade. The performance benchmarks are designed to represent a description of what could be expected from a student in a high-quality performance who has a high degree of understanding of the specific content/concept standard and has consistently experienced the learning actions.

The following template, along with descriptions, is offered as an advance organizer for the performance benchmarks that follow in the next section.

PERFORMANCE BENCHMARK FORMAT

A. FINE ARTS STRAND AND STANDARD NUMBERS		G. TECHNOLOGY ICON
B. KEY ORGANIZING QUESTION:		
C. KEY COMPETENCES	**D. KEY CONCEPTS AND CONTENT**	**E. PERFORMANCE TASKS**
		PERFORMANCE TASK I:
		PERFORMANCE TASK II:
F. QUALITY CRITERIA: "LOOK FORS"		

A. Fine Arts Strand and Standard Numbers

This serves to identify the selected fine arts strand and the specific standard numbers chosen from the content/concept standards pages that precede each set of benchmarks.

B. Key Organizing Question

Each performance benchmark addresses specific content information and is organized around a key organizing question. This question serves as a focusing point for the teacher during the performance. The teacher and student can use these questions to focus attention on the key concept/content and competences required in the performance task.

C. Key Competences

The key competences represent the major learning actions of accessing, interpreting, producing, disseminating, and evaluating. These major learning actions are discussed in detail on the preceding pages.

The actions identified are what the student will *do* with the key concepts and content in this benchmark performance. Those do's or learning actions engage students in demonstrations of competence in technical and social processes. Teachers must teach students how to operationalize these learning actions.

D. Key Concepts and Content

The information contained in this section identifies the major concepts that embrace the essential content and knowledge base that was taught and is now addressed in this performance benchmark. These concepts correspond to the standard numbers in Section A above.

E. Performance Tasks

Each performance task requires students to apply the designated content using specific learning actions they have been taught. This is done in a context or situation related to the key question. The performance tasks can be done individually or collaboratively. In either case, it is still the teacher's responsibility to look for the presence or absence of the quality criteria in action.

There are two performance tasks identified on each performance benchmark page to offer teachers a choice or serve as a parallel task for students. Both tasks correspond to the identified quality criteria.

F. Quality Criteria: "Look fors"

The quality criteria represent key actions that students are expected to demonstrate during the performance task. The criteria also guide the teachers and serve as "look fors" during the performance task. In other words, the teacher observes the students for these specific criteria.

These criteria embody the key competences or learning actions that students should have been taught in preparation for this performance task. Students demonstrate the learning actions in connection to the key concepts.

The criteria serve as a process rubric that guides the design of both instruction and assessment. They also serve as a signpost for the learners.

The criteria are identified following a "do + what" formula, which makes it easy to "look for" them.

G. Technology Icon

The presence of a technology icon at the top of a performance benchmark page means there is a corresponding example in the Technology Connections section. These examples indicate how technologies can assist students in carrying out the key competences required in the performance task.

LISTENING

Content/Concept Standards

Music is an aural art form. If the eye is the window of the soul, then it might be said that the ear is the gateway to the mind and heart. Listening and processing aural information is a form of thinking.

The development of the ability to listen with understanding is essential if students are to gain a broad cultural and historical perspective. In developing listening skills, students should develop the ability to identify various aspects of the composition and ways in which those aspects contribute to the whole work. When students become skilled in hearing "how the music goes," they begin to use their analytical skills developed through purposeful listening to music to understand the form of their works of art.

Listening requires a willingness to approach various types of music with an open mind and to respond to the artistic appeal of music. Because listening to music involves both the mind and the heart (cognitive and affective), it can be wholly absorbing and result in a very rewarding experience.

What students should know how to do by the end of Grade 3

In the early stages of formal music training, students respond to the emotional or feeling dimensions of the music readily and naturally. They interpret the music through movement or with graphic/artistic representations. As they become more familiar with the basic concepts found within music, they begin to conceptualize patterns and formal structures. Young musicians will begin developing critical and analytical skills that form the basis of a deeper understanding and appreciation of music. Students should be able to

1. Identify and describe simple patterns that are used to create form in music
2. Demonstrate an understanding of the basic concepts of melody, accompaniment, and rhythm patterns through listening and discussion
3. Identify the sounds of a variety of instruments and voices, including the major orchestral and band instruments, and adult and children's voices
4. Express through bodily movement selected prominent music characteristics in a given example of a music work
5. Repeat a music idea after having heard it played or sung
6. Recognize the sounds of nature and human-made machines
7. Recognize and verbally explain emotional responses evoked by a piece of music

What students should know how to do by the end of Grade 5

At this critical age, the student engages both verbal and analytical skills to describe and record important life experiences. A deeper understanding of how music works and how a composer uses the elements of music as building blocks gives the student the foundation to experience music as a powerful means of expressing and communicating ideas and feelings. Young musicians are able to recognize the formal qualities of musical works and have developed sufficient vocabulary to articulate their listening experiences. Students should be able to

1. Identify and describe patterns that are used to create form in music
2. Demonstrate an understanding of pitch, duration, intensity, and timbre in an aural example of a work of music
3. Describe specific music elements in a given example of a work of music, using appropriate terminology
4. Differentiate between contrasting sections of a work and their individual characteristics (e.g., "A" section is bold in a strong rhythmic style, and "B" section is gentle and lyrical)
5. Express prominent characteristics in a given example of a music work through bodily movement, both alone and with partners or in small groups
6. Analyze and articulate emotional responses evoked by a piece of music

What students should know how to do by the end of Grade 8

Listening with understanding is an important way for students to learn. Listening improves students' abilities to perform and create music. By the end of Grade 8, students will be familiar with the elements of music and a number of compositional techniques that enable them to identify some of the unifying features of longer and more complex works of music. Another important aspect of developing personal listening skills is the ability to respond emotionally to the artistic qualities of the music. Students should be able to

1. Identify and describe the elements of music, pitch, intensity, duration, timbre, and texture
2. Demonstrate knowledge of the basic principles of meter, rhythm, tonality, intervals, chords, and harmonic progressions
3. Recognize tonal centers and modulations as organizers in music
4. Compare sound textures in the use of voices and/or instruments
5. Differentiate between contrasting sections of a work and categorize a piece of music according to how these sections are organized (e.g., AB [binary], ABA [ternary], ABACAD [rondo], etc.)
6. Investigate the effect that music has on the listeners' behavior, both consciously and subconsciously
7. Describe ways in which works of music can enrich people's lives in such ways as developing self-awareness and insight, providing satisfaction and enjoyment, and engaging the feelings of an individual

What students should know how to do by the end of Grade 12

When composers create works of music, they make use of the materials, techniques, and elements of music. They apply principles of composition that give their works coherence between idea and form, and between form and function. Students should be able to use their listening skills to derive both intellectual and emotional enrichment and personal enjoyment. Students should be able to

1. Analyze examples of works of music (both their own and those of others) in terms of form and structure by describing the uses of the elements of music and expressive devices
2. Deduce that form is reflective of a particular era or genre by listening to examples of works of music
3. Use the technical vocabulary of music to express an understanding of compositional devices, such as unity and variety, tension and release, thematic development, and rhythmic motives
4. Analyze the ways in which different works of music speak to the senses and evoke responses
5. Recognize and explain the common principles of form and structures that exist among the works of various arts

Fine Arts:
Grade 3

Performance
Benchmark

LISTENING
CONTENT/CONCEPT STANDARDS 3 ,6

KEY ORGANIZING QUESTION:

How does noise pollution affect us?

KEY COMPETENCES	KEY CONCEPTS AND CONTENT	PERFORMANCE TASKS
Listen Identify Classify Organize Construct Present Conclude	Focusing on sounds on our environment. Pleasing sounds versus displeasing sounds. Recognizing sounds of nature and human-made machines.	**PERFORMANCE TASK I:** You are the official in charge of the sound environment in your classroom. Make a list of all the sounds you hear and decide whether each sound is pleasing or displeasing. Choose two pleasing sounds and two displeasing sounds, and graph what they might look like on big chart paper. Reproduce the sounds using your voices and any instruments or objects in your classroom. Make a soundscape of about 30 seconds in length that expresses a mood or feeling about your classroom environment using the sounds you have chosen. How do you and your class feel about your classroom sounds? What do you need to change about your sound environment? **PERFORMANCE TASK II:** You are a sound detective. Go outside with your class. Sit alone and listen. Make a list of all of the sounds you hear and decide whether each sound is pleasing or displeasing. Choose two pleasing sounds and two displeasing sounds. Go into your room and graph what they might look like on a piece of chart paper. Reproduce the selected sounds using your voice and any object in your classroom. Make a soundscape of about 30 seconds in length that expresses a mood or feeling about the environment outside your school using the sounds you have chosen. How do you and your classmates feel about your constructed sounds? What should you change about your soundscape?

QUALITY CRITERIA:
"LOOK FORS"

• Clearly state your purpose.
• Remain focused on your task.
• Classify your sounds.
• Select, recreate, organize, and manipulate sounds for presentations.
• Draw conclusions about sounds in your environment.

**Fine Arts:
Grade 5**

LISTENING
CONTENT/CONCEPT STANDARDS 1, 5, 6

KEY ORGANIZING QUESTION:

What is the relationship between the lyrics and the rhythm in a song/poem?

KEY COMPETENCES	KEY CONCEPTS AND CONTENT	PERFORMANCE TASKS
Brainstorm Listen Select Adapt Design Develop Perform Reflect	Listening for the sounds of words and how they fit with music. Responding to the meaning of words and music, and expressing the meaning through song, dance, and visual representation. Selecting and adapting appropriate material for a specific occasion. Music and rhythm as forms of communication.	**PERFORMANCE TASK I:** You will work with a team and be responsible for developing a presentation in celebration of your school's 25th anniversary. First, brainstorm ideas about your school that you want to feature. Then listen to songs that you think offer the right rhythm for your message. Which songs offer lyrics you can adapt? Write your lyrics to fit the notes of your selected song. Make sure your lyrics have a clear meaning and reflect the mood and nature of the music. Develop motions to enhance the meaning of the words and music. Rehearse your song. Have your presentation videotaped. View it with other members of your class. Reflect on your performance and decide what you might do to make the presentation better. **PERFORMANCE TASK II:** You all like your physical education teacher very much and want to give him recognition. In preparation for this event, you must work with a team of students and select a poem that offers an interesting musical beat. Brainstorm interesting ideas about your physical education teacher to include in your work. Adapt the words in the poem to project information about your gym teacher or write a poem of your own. Create a rhythm pattern using percussion instruments, body, and voice sounds that fit the meter of the poem. Practice your piece and then have it videotaped. View it with other members of your class. Reflect on your performance and decide what you could do to make it better. Perform it for your physical education teacher.

**QUALITY CRITERIA:
"LOOK FORS"**

- Clearly state the purpose of your task.
- Review systematically a variety of options.
- Identify key information.
- Develop the information.
- Match the words with the rhythm.
- Develop your routine with actions/sounds.
- Present your finished routine for filming.
- Review your performance.

Fine Arts:
Grade 8

Performance Benchmark

LISTENING
CONTENT/CONCEPT STANDARD 6

KEY ORGANIZING QUESTION:

What effect does background music have on listeners/viewers?

KEY COMPETENCES	KEY CONCEPTS AND CONTENT	PERFORMANCE TASKS
Observe Listen Identify Compare Analyze Select Present Conclude	Music: affects responses and behavior of people. Music: a powerful expression of mood and feeling. Music: enhances the expressive power of other senses. Music: has manipulative qualities even when played as background.	**PERFORMANCE TASK I:** You are the music editor for a movie production. Select a scene from a video/movie (or create your own) and decide what mood the scene evokes. Choose music that shares the same mood. Cue up a portion of that music so that it can be played while the video scene is running. For the sake of comparison, select music that suggests a strongly contrasting mood and play it during the same scene. What reactions did your classmates have with the first selection? What about the second? What conclusions do you have about the effect of music in movies?

QUALITY CRITERIA:
"LOOK FORS"

- State your purpose clearly.
- Select your target focus.
- Note and identify all necessary details.
- Create a scenario that develops opposite effect.
- Analyze the reactions.
- Share your observations and conclusions.

PERFORMANCE TASK II:
Stores use music as a powerful tool to affect shoppers' buying patterns. You have been asked to select music to play over the sound system at the local mall. What will you select? Explain the reasons for your selections. After you play your selections for a test market, change the music and play selections of a contrasting style. Explain the effect of contrasting music on the consumer to another team of students in your class. Share your conclusions with them.

Fine Arts:
Grade 12

Performance
Benchmark

LISTENING
CONTENT/CONCEPT STANDARDS 3, 5

KEY ORGANIZING QUESTION:

How can you use the features of form and structure in music to describe and explain similar features in architecture or literature?

KEY COMPETENCES	KEY CONCEPTS AND CONTENT	PERFORMANCE TASKS
Investigate Listen Examine Compare Contrast Synthesize Evaluate Present	Making connections among art forms in terms of balance, form, and symmetry using: • visual/spatial skills • analytical/ conceptual skills • listening/perceiving skills • verbal/evaluating skills.	**PERFORMANCE TASK I:** You must prepare to guide a tour for a group of Austrian visitors to observe the architectural features of the U.S. Capitol building. You remember that Mozart is their favorite son, so you listen and review the music of Mozart for its symmetry, balance, and form. Write a draft of your presentation on the Capitol's architectural features and include selected listening portions to make key points. Be sure to describe the formal structures in your selected musical portions. Compare them to particular architectural art forms you want to emphasize. Share your planned presentation with a group of your peers. Ask for reactions. Edit your work as you desire and do your final presentation for an American history class. **PERFORMANCE TASK II:** In your literature classes, you may have noted that classical playwrights, such as Shakespeare, build their plays around a three-part form, similar to that of classical music. Investigate the similarities in structures between a classical play and a symphony of your choice. Be sure to note the common qualities. Prepare to share your information with a group of literature students. Write a draft of your presentation and include selected listening portions to make key points. Share your planned presentation with a group of your peers. Ask for their reactions. Edit your work as you desire and do your final presentation for the literature students.

QUALITY CRITERIA:
"LOOK FORS"
• Clearly define your purpose.
• Gather the necessary information from a variety of reliable resources.
• Define the major points for comparing/constrasting.
• Provide accurate, detailed, supporting information.
• Synthesize your findings.
• Present findings and your conclusions.

CREATING

Content/Concept Standards

Playing with sounds and arranging them into interesting patterns is the essence of the creative musical process. Composing involves making choices about sounds in order to achieve a desired effect. Music that makes the listener think and feel is a result of careful crafting.

Creating music provides a challenge to the intellect and imagination. Students should create works of their own so that they learn how and why music is produced. In making choices about sounds, students learn to connect theory with practice, and to articulate the reasons that a work is effective.

What students should know how to do by the end of Grade 3

Young students are keen to experiment with sound. They enjoy selecting sounds that go with a story or illustrate an idea that they have experienced. The teacher must use descriptive, musical terms to help children differentiate sounds as loud or soft, fast or slow, and so forth. A conceptual framework for approaching music creation begins in these early years. Students should be able to

1. Experiment with sounds, purposefully select sounds, and explain choices
2. Use voice, instrument, and found sounds to produce simple accompaniments to familiar songs
3. Compose a piece of music that demonstrates understanding of basic musical concepts (e.g., loud/soft, fast/slow)
4. Use graphic symbols to represent sounds and communicate ideas

What students should know how to do by the end of Grade 5

Students at this age can understand symbol systems and should begin to record the rhythm patterns, melodies, and chord progressions that they create. Teachers should continue to encourage a thoughtful, experimental approach whereby students try out ideas in real sounds, make choices about how to organize sounds, and practice and refine their compositions. As in language development, aural/oral sounds precede the written code for music. Students should be able to

1. Explore, select, and organize sounds to create a piece that has a perceivable, yet simple, musical form
2. Improvise and compose accompaniments that demonstrate an understanding of simple harmony, polyphony, and musical texture
3. Create music that expresses a specific idea or feeling and explain how choices about sound contribute to its effectiveness
4. Use conventional and graphic notation to ensure that rhythm patterns and melody lines can be recalled with accuracy

What students should know how to do by the end of Grade 8

Technology enhances the capacity of students to compose and to notate music. Adolescents need instruction in using computer software and MIDI (musical instrument digital interface) technology to access new sound sources, to input and edit their musical ideas, and to store and print their musical scores. With technology students can apply their understanding of musical concepts and the creative process at greater levels of sound sophistication. Students should be able to

1. Explore electronic, vocal, and instrumental sound sources and select those suitable for expressing specific ideas or feelings
2. Compose a piece demonstrating knowledge of a particular solo instrument or voice

3. Use recording equipment to capture a work in progress and subsequently apply knowledge of music concepts to refine the work

4. Use computer software and MIDI technology to input, edit, store, perform, and print a short piece of music

What students should know how to do by the end of Grade 12

At this stage, students should integrate all the components of musical creativity. They should be able to manipulate the materials of music with ease and to compose effective pieces of music for a variety of performance media. They should be producing a graduation portfolio of polished works, and some compositions should be shared with real audiences. Students should be able to

1. Manipulate a variety of sounds and access sound sources with ease

2. Compose an effective movement or piece in a recognized musical form

3. Produce compositions that demonstrate a sophisticated understanding of musical concepts

4. Demonstrate facility in using computer software and MIDI electronic equipment to notate and record their compositions

Fine Arts: **Performance**
Grade 3   **Benchmark**

CREATING

CONTENT/CONCEPT STANDARD 1

KEY ORGANIZING QUESTION:

What kinds of decisions do composers make?

KEY COMPETENCES	KEY CONCEPTS AND CONTENT	PERFORMANCE TASKS
Gather Listen Choose Organize Create Perform Discuss Perfect Revisit	Composers make choices when they create music, for example: • loud – soft • fast – slow • many sounds – few sounds • strong beat – no beat • long sounds – short sounds • voices – instruments Composers make choices on purpose to have an effect on the listener.	**PERFORMANCE TASK I:** As part of our unit on Being a Friend your group is to create a piece of music that illustrates an emotion like anger, sadness, joy, peacefulness. Choose an emotion and experiment with different voice sounds and instrument sounds. Chose sounds that fit the emotion. Try different ways of arranging the sounds—discuss the effect. Arrange your sounds into a piece of music. Practice and perform it for another group—get their suggestions. Refine your piece and perform it again.

QUALITY CRITERIA:
"LOOK FORS"

- Clearly state your purpose.
- Select your poem or emotion.
- Gather and listen to a variety of sounds.
- Choose sounds purposefully to fit an idea.
- Explain your reasons for your choices.
- Present composition for feedback.
- Refine and perform the composition.

PERF○○

As   Around
the   eate a
sou   poem
that y   then
experi   hear
which ○   ' of
your poe   'if-
ferently f○   v
it sounds
rangement
your arrang○
other group. .
flect on you
necessary cha.
final performanc

Fine Arts:
Grade 5

Performance
Benchmark

CREATING
CONTENT/CONCEPT STANDARD 2

KEY ORGANIZING QUESTION:

How do composers and arrangers create accompaniment for songs?

KEY COMPETENCES	KEY CONCEPTS AND CONTENT	PERFORMANCE TASKS
Choose Organize Discuss Develop Revisit Perform/Present	A song has a melody line. Composers and arrangers create accompaniments for the melody line. Accompaniments may use a variety of sound sources. Accompaniments may result in harmony and polyphony. Different accompaniment choices have different effects.	**PERFORMANCE TASK I:** Your class will be performing a medley of familiar folk songs. Each group is responsible for creating an accompaniment for one of the folk songs. You must include pitched sounds and may include percussion. Choose from among voices, tuned percussion, keyboard, winds, and/or arrange sound sources. Experiment with a variety of ideas and create your accompaniment. Perform it for your peers and incorporate their feedback into revisions. Perfect your piece for public performance.

QUALITY CRITERIA:
"LOOK FORS"

• Identify your purpose.
• Review different possibilities for choosing.
• Experiment with different options.
• Create your arrangement/product.
• Solicit feedback from another group.
• Present your final arrangement/product.

PERFORMANCE TASK II:

Listen to a popular song that is performed by two different recording artists. Make a list of the likenesses and differences you hear in the arrangements. Create a chart comparing the choices each artist/producer made in providing accompaniment and/or backup to the main melody line. Also include choices the artists made in presenting the melody line. On the chart indicate the accompaniment you would make if you were producing the record. Present your detailed chart for a group of your peers in your music class. Explain your choices to them. Have them listen to the two recordings and give you feedback on your choices. Edit your chart as you wish and prepare for a final presentation of the information to your class.

Fine Arts:
Grade 8

CREATING
CONTENT/CONCEPT STANDARDS 1, 3

KEY ORGANIZING QUESTION:
How do composers/producers of music respond to the needs of those who commission (hire) them to create work?

KEY COMPETENCES	KEY CONCEPTS AND CONTENT	PERFORMANCE TASKS
Brainstorm Gather Listen Experiment Organize Create Present Review/Edit	Composers can be hired to create music for specific purposes. The same tools, materials, and processes are used to create music, but filling the client's needs becomes more important than personal choices.	**PERFORMANCE TASK I:** Your school PTA has requested a year-in-review slide show. They have asked your class to create a list of potential slides and to tape a musical collage to be played as the slides are shown. You must work in teams and identify the potential slides. Brainstorm ideas for using various found, vocal, instrumental, or electronic sound sources. As you think of songs or instrumental music, keep in mind the copyright laws. Gather your resources. Plan your musical collage. Try it with a narration of the potential slides; tape the sound track. Listen to it and refine it. Create your final collage to match your slides.

QUALITY CRITERIA:
"LOOK FORS"
• Establish clearly stated purpose.
• Scrutinize a variety of possibilities.
• Make initial selections and listen.
• Try different possibilities.
• Organize a working draft.
• Present for review.
• Edit as necessary.
• Present to identified recipient.

PERFORMANCE TASK II:
As part of the physical education class, students are to create a 4-minute movement sequence to music of your choosing. Meet with the class to ascertain the types, timing, and sequence of movements they wish to incorporate. From a variety of sound sources, create a collage of 4 minutes of music that fits the movement ideas. Present your musical collage to the group of students who are involved in a different movement sequence. Make refinements based on feedback from this group and create your final collage for the physical education class.

**Fine Arts:
Grade 12**

**Performance
Benchmark**

CREATING
CONTENT/CONCEPT STANDARDS 1, 2, 3, 4

KEY ORGANIZING QUESTION:

How do composers use technology?

KEY COMPETENCES	KEY CONCEPTS AND CONTENT	PERFORMANCE TASKS
Select Review Synthesize Organize Compose Publish	Technology can facilitate the mechanical aspects of translating sounds to symbols. Technology can allow the composer to hear the work in progress. Technology is a tool; the composer makes the musical choices.	**PERFORMANCE TASK I:** You are to compose an original piece of music to mark a significant time in life (e.g., graduation, first love, a wedding). Select your focus time of life and identify the performing ensemble. Gather your musical ideas together and review possibilities. Plan and create your original composition. Use technology where it is appropriate. You must produce a printed score of your work using a computer software program (e.g., *Finale, Cakewalk Pro for Windows*). Present your composition to a team of musicians you respect and ask for their reactions and recommendations. Decide if you want to make any changes.

**QUALITY CRITERIA:
"LOOK FORS"**

- Identify your task and the occasion.
- Review relevant possibilities.
- Select important focus features.
- Create a logical sequence.
- Develop a preliminary visual representation.
- Edit or change as needed to meet purpose.
- Publish your final arrangement/score.

PERFORMANCE TASK II:

An instrumental ensemble has asked you to create for them an arrangement of a piano score that they will perform at a school assembly on patriotism. Using computer software (e.g., *Finale, Cakewalk Pro for Windows*) and synthesizers input, arrange your score. Perform it for a team of your peers and solicit their reactions and ideas. Edit as you choose, and publish your final score.

PERFORMING

Content/Concept Standards

Through singing or playing an instrument students can express themselves creatively and learn another way to communicate with one another. By practicing the skills of performance—correct tempo, tone quality and timbre, appropriate style, dynamics, and technique—students may then learn new music independently throughout their lives. Music is a basic and unique part of us and performance exemplifies this.

What students should know how to do by the end of Grade 3

To a large extent students from kindergarten to Grade 3 learn by doing. Performing by singing and playing musical instruments enables the students to express themselves freely. Students in this formative stage must learn the basic concepts of a good musical performance. Students should be able to

1. Perform independently displaying good pitch, correct tempo and rhythm, expressiveness, and appropriate style
2. Perform in groups blending voices, matching dynamic levels, and responding to cues of conductor
3. Perform a song in unison, in a round, or with a partner
4. Explain and evaluate the major components of a good music performance

What students should know how to do by the end of Grade 5

Students must perform music in a variety of musical styles. The music performed should exhibit quality, tone, technique, and expression. Experience in performing a wide variety of music will enable students to make informed musical judgments. Students should be able to

1. Perform alone displaying good breath control, expression, and rhythmic and technical accuracy in a variety of musical styles
2. Perform in larger ensembles and in two parts music from various cultures and genres displaying good blend, expressiveness, and responding to cues of the conductor
3. Assess the quality of their own and other's performance by applying specific criteria appropriate for the style of music

What students should know how to do by the end of Grade 8

Students can express themselves creatively through performing a wide variety of music. Students must exhibit a knowledge of music notation and musical styles in solo and group performance. Students must be able to evaluate a performance in appropriate terms. Students should be able to

1. Perform alone a wide variety of music with expression, technical accuracy, rhythmic vitality, and in various musical styles
2. Perform in large group with at least three (3) parts displaying good blend, expressiveness, and responding to cues of the conductor
3. Sight read in a variety of styles
4. Evaluate self and peers in performance using appropriate music criteria and language

What students should know how to do by the end of Grade 12

Students are encouraged to develop a sense of personal expression in the performing of music. Students must exhibit quality tone, expression, and technique and style in the performance of solos, chamber music, large ensembles, and in sight reading. The ability to evaluate their own performances and those of others is an important skill. Students should be able to

1. Select and perform solo repertoire with accompaniment where suitable

2. Perform in small ensembles with a maximum of two (2) to a part

3. Perform in large ensembles, blending timbres, matching dynamic levels and intonation, and responding to the cues of a conductor

4. Sight read and interpret music notation in a variety of styles

5. Evaluate a performance by applying selected criteria and using appropriate terminology

Fine Arts:
Grade 3

PERFORMING
CONTENT/CONCEPT STANDARDS 2, 3, 4

KEY ORGANIZING QUESTION:

What do you do when you learn a piece of music that has two distinct parts?

KEY COMPETENCES	KEY CONCEPTS AND CONTENT	PERFORMANCE TASKS
Listen Sing Rehearse Combine Perform Assess	Learn a two-part song. Perform with dynamics, blending voices, and by watching cues of conductor.	**PERFORMANCE TASK I:** Your class is going to celebrate learning by having everyone invite their parents or a special guest to the classroom. As part of the program, the students will sing rounds of *Row, Row, Row Your Boat*. To get ready for this you must learn all the words to the song and tape it. Listen to the tape and try singing the second round of the song as you listen to the first round. Tell a learning partner what you must do to sing in the right words in the right round of the song. When your teacher has the class singing the three rounds, tape it. Listen to the tape and explain to a friend how the song sounds and how you feel about it.

QUALITY CRITERIA:
"LOOK FORS"

- Clearly state your purpose.
- Remain focused on the song.
- Listen carefully to the rounds.
- Sing and rehearse the parts.
- Perform and record the song.
- Assess your actions and feelings.

PERFORMANCE TASK II:

As part of a cultural event at your school, your class is going to learn the main theme of *Haida* by Henry Leck. Once it can be sung confidently, divide the song into parts as a round. Add movements as indicated in the score. Tape your song in parts and listen to the tape. Explain to a friend how the song sounds to you and how you feel about it. Also tell your partner what you must do to remain on the right words in the right round of the song.

Fine Arts:
Grade 5

Performance
Benchmark

PERFORMING
CONTENT/CONCEPT STANDARD 1

KEY ORGANIZING QUESTION:

How do you perform a simple melody in various styles employing all the aspects of a quality performance?

KEY COMPETENCES	KEY CONCEPTS AND CONTENT	PERFORMANCE TASKS
Select Organize Practice Perform Listen Respond	Design a solo performance of a simple song in various styles with good tone quality, expression, and technical and rhythmic accuracy.	**PERFORMANCE TASK I:** You have been asked to perform in a local music festival, which is focusing on performances by individual students. You must select a simple song such as *Twinkle, Twinkle Little Star* and explore several variations of the song. Select the variations you like best and design several variations of your own. Then practice your performance. Present your variations to a group of your peers and ask them to judge you on quality of performance and the overall effectiveness of the various styles presented. Listen and make changes as you desire.

QUALITY CRITERIA:
"LOOK FORS"

- Identify your purpose.
- Review possible choices or variations.
- Classify your selections.
- Layout your short program in logical order.
- Rehearse and present your sequence.
- Adjust to responses as desired.

PERFORMANCE TASK II:
You are attending a birthday party for a friend, and you must be prepared to present the Birthday Song in several variations. Select possible variations, practice them and then present them to another friend before the official party. Ask your friend to judge you on quality of performance and the overall effectiveness of the various styles you presented. Listen and make changes as you desire. Practice your renditions and prepare to present them to the birthday person.

Fine Arts:
Grade 8

PERFORMING
CONTENT/CONCEPT STANDARD 3

KEY ORGANIZING QUESTION:

How does the professional singer or orchestral musician approach sight reading?

KEY COMPETENCES	KEY CONCEPTS AND CONTENT	PERFORMANCE TASKS
Select Review Organize Design Conduct Review Publish	Patterns in approaching a piece of sight reading. All music has elements that make sight reading easier.	**PERFORMANCE TASK I:** You must teach a group of fifth graders to sight read a piece of music. Select a piece of music and review the elements of the piece that must be observed to ensure a quality performance. Organize the elements into a logical order and develop a system that will help you remember these elements. Design a guide for the fifth-grade students that will help them apply your strategies when they are asked to sight read a number. Use your guide with several students to see if they find it helpful. Listen to their reactions and make necessary changes to your guide. Publish your final draft and make it available to others.

QUALITY CRITERIA:
"LOOK FORS"

- Clearly articulate your task.
- Survey the details of the selected piece.
- Identify the key elements.
- Arrange elements in a logical sequence.
- Create a usable plan.
- Exercise your plan with a selected group.
- Review and adjust as needed.

PERFORMANCE TASK II:
You are going to lead a group of students through a sight reading session on a selected new piece of music. Review the music first and identify the elements into a logical order and develop a system for remembering them. Design a lesson plan you can use with your group. Be sure to include the necessary strategies they need to apply when sight reading the music. Clearly convey your strategies to the group. Lead them through the experience and ask them for their reactions. Make the necessary changes to your approach and try it again. Publish your lesson plan for others to use.

Fine Arts:
Grade 12

PERFORMING
CONTENT/CONCEPT STANDARD 5

KEY ORGANIZING QUESTION:

How is a critical judgment of a musical performance communicated?

KEY COMPETENCES	KEY CONCEPTS AND CONTENT	PERFORMANCE TASKS
Identify Compare Contrast Discuss Conclude	Listening: Tone Expression Style Technique Interpretation	**PERFORMANCE TASK I:** You must listen to a performance of *Spring* from *The Four Seasons* by Vivaldi. Identify and apply what you know about a quality performance, and write a short review of the performance you heard using the appropriate music terminology. Would you recommend this recording to the public and why? When you have completed your review, read a review of the same performance by a professional critic. Compare the similarities and differences between the two critiques. Discuss them with a classmate. Draw your own conclusions and present them to a committee of your peers.

QUALITY CRITERIA:
"LOOK FORS"

- Identify your purpose.
- Review important concepts and vocabulary.
- Closely examine key points or elements.
- Select items for comparison.
- Select major differences with others.
- Expand ideas through discussion.
- Arrange the ideas and necessary details.
- Review and refine as needed.
- Draw conclusions.

PERFORMANCE TASK II:
You are going to assist others in listening critically to a musical performance. You need to identify key criteria for a quality performance using appropriate music terminology. Your criteria should help the listener decide whether they could recommend the performance or recording. When you have completed your criteria checklist, compare it with the list of a fellow student. Discuss the similarities and the differences between the two sets of criteria. Draw your own conclusions and refine your criteria list. Ask friends to use it as they listen to a musical performance. Have them report back to you their reactions to your criteria list.

MUSIC IN RELATION TO ART

Content/Concept Standards

The Arts are an effective vehicle for communication. We learn through our senses and we can show what we know through music, visual arts, drama, and dance. The Arts in combination with technology result in powerful media messages.

The concepts and language of music relate to those in other areas. Form, symmetry, balance, pattern, dynamics, rhythm, texture, sound, and symbol are ideas shared with mathematics, science, dance, drama, visual arts, and technology.

Music and the Arts speak to our emotions, feed our souls, and illuminate our experiences. Works of art help us to consider familiar things in a new way and alert us to the human condition.

Through music and the Arts, students develop the skills needed to work with others and to contribute to their community. They learn to concentrate, to refine their practice, and to display their achievements.

What students should know how to do by the end of Grade 3

Younger students must make a connection between musical and arts activities and their own life experiences. Songs, paintings, stories, dance, and role-play should weave in and out of topics of interest to the students. It is important that teachers use an arts vocabulary in naming the child's experiences and point out where arts are found in life outside of school. Students should be able to

1. Explore ideas and feelings through songs, paintings, movement, and role-plays
2. Communicate messages found in different types of artworks
3. Describe basic musical concepts using appropriate vocabulary
4. Describe or demonstrate personal responses to works of music, dance, drama, and visual arts
5. Identify knowledge and skills gained through arts activities and explain how they are important to life

What students should know how to do by the end of Grade 5

As students begin to become aware of aspects of life outside of their own direct experience, they should begin to use the Arts as a means of learning and communicating about the world. As young consumers, students need to understand how music and the Arts affect their feelings and behavior and how advertisers rely on the Arts to influence people. Students should be able to find examples of arts elements and techniques across the curriculum. Students should be able to

1. Express ideas and demonstrate learning from a variety of subject areas through the Arts
2. Identify various arts materials and media that are used to convey messages in advertisements and commercial art
3. Provide examples of musical concepts and vocabulary that apply to other subject areas
4. Differentiate between emotional and intellectual responses to works of music, dance, drama, and visual arts
5. Demonstrate conventional behavior as performer or audience member at arts events

What students should know how to do by the end of Grade 8

Adolescents are generally quite engaged in popular youth culture. The challenge is to bring them to an understanding of how powerful music, dance, drama, and visual arts are as vehicles for influencing thought and actions. In addition, adolescents must be encouraged to participate in the range of cultural life in the community. Students should be able to

1. Provide information and perspectives on issues and topics under study using works of music, dance, drama, and visual arts

2. Create artworks that convey persuasive messages using elements of the arts (e.g., sound, images, movement)

3. Describe aesthetic qualities of natural and human-made objects and materials (e.g., form, balance, color)

4. Give evidence that works of art can direct attention to social, political, and cultural conditions

5. Participate in and contribute to the cultural life of the community using arts knowledge and skills

What students should know how to do by the end of Grade 12

Senior students should demonstrate facility in using music and the Arts to enrich their own life, to communicate powerful ideas and feelings, and to enhance their abilities to make sense of the world. Students should be able to

1. Convey and interpret meaning with clarity and precision across the curriculum using arts knowledge and techniques

2. Create an effective media campaign using skills and materials from the arts and technology

3. Produce and evaluate products in various areas of life using aesthetic criteria

4. Identify and describe ways in which specific works of art can affect people's attitudes to social, political, and cultural conditions, and can influence their actions

5. Identify and describe occupations where skills developed through the Arts are important, and assess personal artistic abilities in relation to various arts-related employment options

Fine Arts:
Grade 3

Performance
Benchmark

MUSIC IN RELATION TO ART
CONTENT/CONCEPT STANDARDS 1, 4

KEY ORGANIZING QUESTION:
How can you use the Arts to focus our thoughts, feelings, and energy?

KEY COMPETENCES	KEY CONCEPTS AND CONTENT	PERFORMANCE TASKS
Find Choose Develop Present Reflect Revisit	The Arts can express and provoke human thoughts and feelings. Exposure to works of art can affect people's energy level. The arts can be used to alter our behaviors.	**PERFORMANCE TASK I:** Your parents will be visiting the school and you are to present a short story to them. Consider the ideas, feelings, and energy level of the story. Find sounds, songs, and instrumental music; colors, shapes, and paintings; gestures, movements, and dance steps that fit the story. Experiment using these to help the storytelling be more effective. Make decisions about what you will use. Practice your presentation. Use feedback from your peers to refine your work. **PERFORMANCE TASK II:** Your class has been asked by the principal to choose pieces of music to be played at key times during the school day. She wants pieces that will help students concentrate, move in an orderly fashion, become energized, and become physically calmer. Using your knowledge of how your peers respond to different musical selections, select two pieces for each of the four items in her request. Use feedback from your peers to refine your work.

QUALITY CRITERIA:
"LOOK FORS"
• Identify your purpose.
• Identify possibilities.
• Select story, art, and music that enhance ideas and feelings.
• Arrange ideas in logical sequence.
• Rehearse presentation.
• Identify areas for improving.

Fine Arts:
Grade 5

MUSIC IN RELATION TO ART
CONTENT/CONCEPT STANDARD 2

KEY ORGANIZING QUESTION:

How can arts be used to influence consumers?

KEY COMPETENCES	KEY CONCEPTS AND CONTENT	PERFORMANCE TASKS
Investigate Examine Design Develop Analyze Conclude Broadcast	The Arts speak directly to the feelings and can influence behaviors. Advertisers use the Arts to connect their products to human emotions and desires. Knowing how the Arts are used to sell a product can help consumers cut through the hype.	**PERFORMANCE TASK I:** To be a wise consumer, you need to separate information from hype. Investigate a product that many people purchase or use and examine the advertising used to market it. Look at the activities, the sights, the sounds/music that are used in the advertisement. How do they relate to the product and to your own life experiences? What actual information about the product is presented? Analyze your findings and draw conclusions about the effectiveness of the advertising. Broadcast your information and conclusions on your school television network.

QUALITY CRITERIA:
"LOOK FORS"

- Identify your purpose and your audience.
- Delineate the difference between hype and important information.
- Select appropriate information and materials to suit your purpose.
- Create a detailed script.
- Review the content and the delivery.
- Tie conclusion to original purpose.
- Organize the text and support materials.
- Record on video and reflect on the results.

PERFORMANCE TASK II:
Is there too much waste in the lunchroom, or are the school grounds covered with litter? Identify and investigate a problem that exists in your school. Examine the problem and determine the message that needs to be delivered to your school community. Design and develop an advertising campaign that addresses the problem. Be sure to include activities, sights, sounds/music in your campaign. Analyze your campaign and draw conclusions from the reactions and behaviors of the students. Videotape and broadcast your message and findings on the school television network.

**Fine Arts:
Grade 8**

**Performance
Benchmark**

MUSIC IN RELATION TO ART
CONTENT/CONCEPT STANDARD 5

KEY ORGANIZING QUESTION:

What do people need to know to be comfortable participants in the musical and arts life of the community?

KEY COMPETENCES	KEY CONCEPTS AND CONTENT	PERFORMANCE TASKS
Obtain Classify Organize Develop Share Publish	Participation in the arts life of a community is everyone's right. There are a variety of choices in most communities of size. With different arts events come different sets of expectations for the audiences. Information on how to participate and knowing the expected dress and behaviors are helpful to the public.	**PERFORMANCE TASK I:** Your class will be developing a guide for arts audiences in your community. Obtain information about the various arts events and venues. Classify them accordingly and organize into specific categories for various audiences. Include all the necessary information about location, costs, seating, and so forth. Share with the readers your recommendations about dress code and expected behaviors. Organize your collected information into a usable community handbook and publish for distribution. **PERFORMANCE TASK II:** A professional theater group is planning to perform a children's matinee at your school. They are expecting all the students to be knowledgable about the story line and to be prepared with appropriate behaviors and reactions. Your class must obtain all of the necessary information and organize it for your student body. Develop recommendations for students of different ages about the appropriate behaviors and reactions. Provide them with necessary information on the story line so they will be prepared for the performance. Publish your recommended ideas and procedures and distribute to all the classes.

**QUALITY CRITERIA:
"LOOK FORS"**

- Establish clearly stated goals.
- Clarify the needed information.
- Classify and organize according to purpose.
- Identify a possible approach for various events.
- Arrange all needed details.
- Include visual arts in your published product.
- Distribute a quality product to your intended audience.

Fine Arts:
Grade 12

MUSIC IN RELATION TO ART
CONTENT/CONCEPT STANDARD 4

KEY ORGANIZING QUESTION:

How do artists use their skills and knowledge to influence societal change?

KEY COMPETENCES	KEY CONCEPTS AND CONTENT	PERFORMANCE TASKS
Select Research Analyze Choose Develop Present Evaluate	The role of the artist, musician, dancer, and actor is to feel deeply, to think critically, and to act on their thoughts and feelings. The Arts can serve as agents of change by providing and provoking critique of current affairs.	**PERFORMANCE TASK I:** As concerned citizens with skills in the Arts, you will create works of art designed to influence attitudes and motivate people to act to solve a community health and safety issue: • Select an issue to highlight. • Research, analyze, and refine the issue. • Choose an artistic medium—song, sculpture, dance, multimedia. • Develop your work—gather feedback as to its effectiveness as you progress. • With others, find venues for sharing your works. • Set up displays and stage performances. • Evaluate the effectiveness of your products. **PERFORMANCE TASK II:** As part of a study on issues in American history, select a topic or theme (e.g., women's roles, war, rich and poor) that has evolved over the years. Research and find pieces of music, art, dance, or drama that depict or critique the state of affairs in this country in relation to the topic you have chosen. Analyze your own feelings on this topic. Determine how you can draw public attention to this topic through the Arts. Choose a medium, then design and develop a product to convey your message. You want to draw audience attention to your views as expressed through your art. Present your work at a public showing. Evaluate the effectiveness. Did you evoke reactions or feelings among your viewers?

QUALITY CRITERIA:
"LOOK FORS"

• Identify a clear purpose.
• Utilize a variety of reliable resources.
• Organize information.
• Communicate issue clearly and effectively through artistic medium.
• Successfully deliver the artistic message to your selected audience.

MUSIC IN RELATION TO HISTORY/WORLD CULTURES

Content/Concept Standards

Music more than any other art form reflects the diverse cultures of our population. Music is as varied as the cultures that create it. All people from the earliest of times have created music. Music communicates a feeling and speaks to the inner self. It is crucial for young musicians to learn of their own musical heritage and their music history and culture of others so they too can be in touch with the inner being.

What students should know how to do by the end of Grade 3

At a young age, children are intrigued by all types of music: classical, popular, jazz. As well, they are fascinated by stories of composers and music from different parts of the world. It is essential that their natural curiosity be satisfied in such a way that they will continue to want to know more about their musical culture and music history. Students should be able to

1. Identify by kind or style several examples of music from various historical periods and cultures
2. Describe simply how music varies between different cultures
3. Identify uses of music in day-to-day experiences and describe characteristics that make certain music suitable for each use
4. Identify and describe roles of musicians in various music settings and cultures
5. Demonstrate appropriate audience behavior in different music settings

What students should know how to do by the end of Grade 5

Students who understand how culture and history shape social attitudes and behaviors are better equipped to live and work in our increasingly multicultural society. When students are introduced to a wide variety of music from many different sources, they will realize that there are many devices that unify all music. Students should be able to

1. Illustrate how music in a certain time or place reflects social, cultural, and economic conditions
2. Describe how musical style is influenced by culture, society, and technology
3. Compare and connect the function of music in several cultures of the world and the role of musicians in these societies
4. Connect personal experience in music with those of other cultures

What students should know how to do by the end of Grade 8

Music reflects different times in history, and the importance of various peoples and cultures in that development are important links. Students should realize how music influences and how it has been used throughout history. Students should be able to

1. Describe distinguishing characteristics of music from different eras and cultures
2. Compare in several world cultures the function that music serves, roles of musicians, and conditions under which music is performed
3. Describe music that reflects different world cultures
4. Classify by genre and style a wide range of musical works and explain the role and importance of each

What students should know how to do by the end of Grade 12

Every music era and music of various cultures has a distinctive character. When we hear music of a particular historical period or a certain country, we experience the feeling and style of the time or place. Music is a tangible way to touch and be touched by our human heritage. It puts us in contact with those who lived before us or who live at the same time yet in a different part of our world. It is crucial that students make these connections. Students should be able to

1. Classify by genre and style and by historical period or culture a wide variety of music and explain their classification

2. Identify and explain the form and special traits of a given musical work and define its place in history and culture

3. Identify and describe music styles that show the influence of two or more cultural traditions. Identify the connections and trace the historical conditions that made the connections evident

4. Trace the evolution of American music and discover the well-known musicians associated with this music

Fine Arts:
Grade 3

MUSIC IN RELATION TO HISTORY/WORLD CULTURES
CONTENT/CONCEPT STANDARD 2

KEY ORGANIZING QUESTION:

How does music from different cultures vary and how is it the same?

KEY COMPETENCES	KEY CONCEPTS AND CONTENT	PERFORMANCE TASKS
Select Listen Compare Contrast Sketch Draw Present	A wide variety of music from different parts of the world have many of the same traits. Basic musical elements. Distinctive parts of certain music.	**PERFORMANCE TASK I:** You must design a booth for a cultural fair. Select a country of your choice and listen to music representing that culture. Compare and contrast the different patterns you are able to identify. Sketch and draw a decorated cultural fair booth for this country. Present your sketches and drawings to your class along with the selected music. Have your classmates identify the culture. Ask them to explain the reasons for their choices. **PERFORMANCE TASK II:** In small groups, select music from three distinctly different cultures. Listen carefully to the music then identify unique patterns. Compare and contrast the patterns you identified from each culture. Sketch and draw a picture that you think represents the music of each culture. Present your set of pictures to another group of students. Have them listen to the music and match it correctly with your drawings. Ask them to explain the reasons for their matches.

QUALITY CRITERIA:
"LOOK FORS"

• Clearly define your purpose.
• Remain focused on music when listening.
• Identify significant patterns.
• Select points that are similar.
• Select points that are different.
• Create a rough draft for your project.
• Include necessary unique features.
• Develop final draft with details.
• Present ideas and materials to selected audience.

Fine Arts:
Grade 5

MUSIC IN RELATION TO HISTORY/WORLD CULTURES
CONTENT/CONCEPT STANDARD 1

KEY ORGANIZING QUESTION:

How is war reflected in music?

KEY COMPETENCES	KEY CONCEPTS AND CONTENT	PERFORMANCE TASKS
Investigate Identify Analyze Select Plan Arrange Sing	The reflection of social, cultural, and economic conditions in music.	**PERFORMANCE TASK I:** Your class is responsible for a school assembly to honor the men and women who lost their lives in wars that have involved our nation. You must investigate several wars and identify various songs written during those times of war. Listen to the various songs and analyze them for influences of the time, place, and relationship to the economy and society. Select the songs you will sing and/or use in your assembly. Plan your program and hold your assembly to honor the war fatalities. **PERFORMANCE TASK II:**

QUALITY CRITERIA:
"LOOK FORS"

- Clearly state your purpose.
- Gather accurate information from various resources.
- Identify main ideas.
- Identify and discuss relationships.
- Organize your discoveries and ideas.
- Interact with the message through song and media.
- Organize the program and produce it.

Your class is investigating war through the music of the time. Identify several veterans or historians in your area and arrange to interview them. In addition to their general information, ask them to share specific songs that reflect their war. Listen to their stories and their music and analyze for influence of the time, place, and relationship to the economy and society. Select stories and music to use in a program for another class. Select songs you can sing and stories you can relate. Plan your program on wartime reflections and arrange for the other class to visit.

Fine Arts: **Performance**
Grade 8   **Benchmark**

MUSIC IN RELATION TO HISTORY/WORLD CULTURES
CONTENT/CONCEPT STANDARD 1

KEY ORGANIZING QUESTION:

How do you distinguish between music of the Baroque period and music of the Classical period?

KEY COMPETENCES	KEY CONCEPTS AND CONTENT	PERFORMANCE TASKS
Research Evaluate Plan Record Design Write Reflect	Music representing two historical periods. Musical traits of period music.	**PERFORMANCE TASK I:** You are going to serve as a musical adviser for an ambassador who will be entertaining various heads of state at a formal dinner party. The host has requested that music from the Baroque and Classical periods be used throughout the entire evening from the entrance of the guests, through dinner, and for a musical presentation after the meal. You must research these two musical periods and evaluate the music for your selections. Plan and record your evening selections on a tape. Design a program for the gala event and include explanations for your selections. Share your tape with several professionals and seek their reactions. **PERFORMANCE TASK II:** The local symphony is soliciting suggested programs for an evening of musical pleasure from the Baroque and the Classical periods. As a musical adviser, research these two musical periods and evaluate the music for your suggested program. Plan for the evening of listening and make a recording of your suggested program. Design a visual program for the symphony guests and be sure to include written explanations and highlights of your recommendations. Share your tape with the program director of the symphony and ask for input.

QUALITY CRITERIA:
"LOOK FORS"
• Identify your purpose.
• Utilize a variety of resources.
• Identify potential musical pieces.
• Carefully examine the details of your selections.
• Create a draft of your audiotape.
• Assemble the audiotape.
• Arrange ideas and visuals for the program.
• Publish a graphic representation of your program.
• Reflect on the materials and the impact on an audience.

Fine Arts:
Grade 12

Performance
Benchmark

MUSIC IN RELATION TO HISTORY/WORLD CULTURES
CONTENT/CONCEPT STANDARDS 1, 2

KEY ORGANIZING QUESTION:

How does music communicate distinct characteristics of a time, place, or culture?

KEY COMPETENCES	KEY CONCEPTS AND CONTENT	PERFORMANCE TASKS
Investigate Analyze Translate Design Develop Review Broadcast	Genre and style of historical periods or cultures. Special traits of music.	**PERFORMANCE TASK I:** As a musical adviser for an educational production company, you must investigate a particular social, cultural, or economic theme/issue from our country's past. As you analyze your selected theme or issue, translate the information through selected works of art and musical pieces. Design and develop a script for a video that could be used to teach important historical concepts through the communicative power of music and visual art. Review your script and your ideas with a committee of your peers. Make necessary adjustments and then produce your video and arrange to broadcast it over a local cable channel for members of the community or a selected audience.

QUALITY CRITERIA:
"LOOK FORS"

- Identify your purpose.
- Research a variety of reliable resources.
- Organize gathered information into main ideas.
- Identify key concepts.
- Relate to visual and audio ideas.
- Organize information logically/clearly.
- Tie conclusion to original purpose.
- Revisit ideas and information with others.
- Create an appealing, informative product for transmitting.

PERFORMANCE TASK II:
You are a producer who will investigate two cultures, the music of those cultures, and the role music played in those cultures. As you analyze the gathered information on your two cultures, translate your ideas into a story line for a video that would trace the role music played in the two centuries. If possible, identify connections or dramatic differences between the two settings. Design and develop your video script and review it with a selected committee. Make necessary adjustments in your script and then produce the video. Arrange to broadcast it over your community cable channel.

3
TECHNOLOGY CONNECTIONS

SUMMARY

Why Address Technology in a Performance-Based Curriculum?

A performance-based curriculum starts with the understanding that students will make use of what they learn in the production and dissemination of knowledge. Technology is revolutionizing the way we access information; the capabilities we have in interpreting and analyzing data; the methods by which we produce, design, and construct products resulting from our learning; the forms those products take; the methods by which the products are disseminated; and the evaluation procedures we can undertake. *Access, interpret, produce, disseminate,* and *evaluate:* These are the five central learning actions in a performance-based curriculum. These learning actions used in conjunction with technology give the learner more power and lead to greater effectiveness.

PERFORMANCE-BASED LEARNING ACTIONS WHEEL

Technology as Content

Our physical, social, and material worlds are being radically changed as a result of the explosion of new technologies. Technological change and the issues stemming from that change provide content that is increasingly addressed in the study of history, economics, political science, and other disciplines making up the social sciences. They are also subject matter for novels, science fiction, and political and social essays. Technology is a central focus of futuristic studies. It is a product of, as well as a critical ingredient in, modern science. Technological developments have radically altered the tools used by authors and everyone involved in communication and the use of language. Technology is a rich source of topics for integrating a performance-based curriculum.

Technology as a Tool

Technology is also used as a tool in a performance-based curriculum. Although technology can be used as a way of controlling the learner's interaction with the curriculum, technology is most appropriately used as a tool controlled by the learner in the performance-based approach to learning. It is that approach that is applied in correlating this section with the Fine Arts performance benchmarks.

Many technologies can enhance a performance-based curriculum. Their common characteristic is that they are tools that improve communication of and access to multimedia data (words, numbers, sounds, still and motion pictures, still and motion graphics) and make the use of those data easier and more effective. In a perfect world, every student and teacher would have a workstation equipped with a computer, modem, CD-ROM, laserdisc player, a digital camera, and a videotape camera and player. This workstation would be connected to networks that allow access to multimedia data on demand. The networks would distribute information in multimedia format to others throughout the world. In addition to these workstations, teachers and learners would have access to copying, scanning, and printing machines; CD-ROM presses; video editing equipment; audio recording and editing equipment; and software to support writing, computer-aided design, statistics, graphing, musical and artistic productions, and so on. Additional equipment would be found in a science laboratory, including tools for specialized data collection and analysis. In other specialty areas, such as art, lithographic presses would be available. Drafting equipment, electronic tools, and other specialized technologies would be present where necessary to allow the teaching of those technological subject areas.

Technology is a tool (among other tools) useful for acquiring, storing, manipulating, and communicating information in a multimedia format. Technology will be used to gather data, explore questions, produce products, and communicate results.

Technology in Support of Learning Actions

Five learning actions are central to a performance-based curriculum: **ACCESS**, **INTERPRET**, **PRODUCE**, **DISSEMINATE**, and **EVALUATE**. Throughout this curriculum framework, the use of appropriate technologies will support students in being active learners. Students will be encouraged to use technology to generate questions and identify problems in a wide variety of contexts; formulate hypotheses and generate tentative solutions to the questions or the problems they have defined; test the reasonableness of their answers and respond to challenges to their positions; reach a conclusion about an issue, a problem, or a question and use that "solution" as a jumping-off place to ask other questions; and engage in the learning process again.

A learner with a purpose, an issue, a question, or an idea needs to be able to use appropriate technologies in carrying out these learning actions. Technology is especially important in accessing information, producing products, and disseminating the results of one's work. We organize the benchmarks of the skills students must have in using technology around these key learning actions that can take full advantage of current technologies: **ACCESS**, **PRODUCE**, and **DISSEMINATE**. Examples have been developed for some strands at each of the grade levels. Each example contains suggestions on how to use technology to **ACCESS** information, **PRODUCE** products, and **DISSEMINATE** the results of one's efforts. These examples are meant to stimulate and facilitate the mastery of the use of appropriate technologies in the pursuit of learning. The suggested technologies encompass a broad range of tools useful in accessing, producing, and disseminating data that are not just words and numbers but are also sounds, still and motion graphics, and still and motion pictures. Students and teachers are encouraged to use all appropriate tools and disseminate their products using a combination of technologies.

Technology changes rapidly. The skills and abilities described below require modification on a regular basis to reflect the latest technologies. These skills and abilities must be understood as dynamic objectives rather than as static goals. They are essential learning actions that increase the student's ability to **ACCESS**, **PRODUCE**, and **DISSEMINATE**.

SKILLS AND ABILITIES

How students should be able to use technology by the end of Grade 3

Access:

A1	Gather information with still, digital, or video camera
A2	Search databases to locate information
A3	Gather sounds and conversations with audio and video recorders
A4	Collect digitized audio data
A5	Access information on laserdisc by using bar code reader
A6	Scan to capture graphic data
A7	Copy to gather graphics
A8	Retrieve and print information using a computer
A9	Gather information through telephone
A10	Select and use information from CDs
A11	Fax to send and receive printed information
A12	Identify and use all types of materials, such as print, nonprint, and electronic media
A13	Locate information using electronic indexes or media

Produce:

P1	Draw and paint graphics and pictures using a computer
P2	Create flip card animations using a computer
P3	Design and develop computer products including pictures, photographs, text, flip card animations, sounds, and graphics
P4	Design and develop audiotapes
P5	Design and develop videotapes
P6	Create overhead or slide presentations with or without background music
P7	Develop stories using computer-generated text with either handmade or computer-generated illustrations

Disseminate:

D1	Present *Logo* or *HyperCard* (or similar) computer product including pictures, text, flip card animations, sounds, and graphics
D2	Publish printed page including text and graphics
D3	Broadcast audiotape
D4	Broadcast videotape
D5	Present overhead or slide presentation
D6	Fax information to other audiences
D7	Explain products or creations to an audience

How students should be able to use technology by the end of Grade 5

Access:

A1   Gather information with a still, digital, or video camera of moderate complexity

A2   Gather information using text-based databases to locate information

A3   Access information on laserdisc by using bar code reader and computer controls

A4   Gather information using telephone and modem to connect to other users and databases (Internet, eWorld, etc.)

A5   Search basic library technologies for data

A6   Select and use specialized tools appropriate to grade level and subject matter

A7   Record interviews with experts

A8   Scan CD collections for needed information

Produce:

P1   Create path-based animations using computer

P2   Create with computer painting and drawing tools of moderate complexity

P3   Digitize still and motion pictures

P4   Create basic spreadsheet for addition, subtraction, multiplication, and division

P5   Graph data (pie charts, line and bar graphs) using computer

P6   Create edited videotapes of moderate complexity using a videotape editing deck or computer-based digital editing system or two connected cassette recorders (VCRs)

P7   Input text into computer using keyboard with appropriate keyboard skills

P8   Design and develop moderately complex *Logo* or *HyperCard* (or similar) programs including pictures, photographs, sounds, flip card and path-based animations, graphics, text, and motion pictures

P9   Design and develop multipage document including text and graphics using computer

P10   Create edited audiotape

P11   Create edited videotape

P12   Create overhead or slide presentation with synchronized voice narration with or without background music

P13   Lay out advertisements, posters, and banners

Disseminate:

D1   Present moderately complex *Logo* or *HyperCard* (or similar) computer product including pictures, sounds, flip card and path-based animations, graphics, text, and motion pictures

D2   Publish multipage printed document including formatted, paginated text and graphics

D3   Broadcast edited audiotape and videotape

D4   Present programs using overhead projector, slide projector, or computer

D5   Present information over public address system in a school, community, or meeting situation

D6   Display information in a variety of formats

D7   Advertise for events, services, or products

D8   Broadcast performances and products

D9   Broadcast on cable TV

How students should be able to use technology by the end of Grade 8

Access:

A1   Gather information using computer, CD-ROM, and laserdisc databases

A2   Gather data using telephone and modem (including graphics and sounds) to and from other users and databases (Internet, eWorld, etc.)

A3   Search basic spreadsheet and databasing software for "what if?" comparisons and analyses

A4   Search technologies for accessing data outside the school and local library

A5   Search menus to locate information on computer software, CD-ROM, or laserdiscs

A6   Video interviews

A7   Download information from Internet

Produce:

P1   Create products using computer painting and drawing tools, including moderately complex color tools

P2   Digitize still and motion pictures

P3   Create edited videotapes by using a videotape editing deck or computer-based digital editing system

P4   Create computer presentation program

P5   Develop cell-based animations using computer

P6   Design and develop complex *Logo* or *HyperCard* (or similar) programs including still pictures; photographs; flip card, path-based, and cell-based animations; sounds; graphics; and motion pictures

P7   Create multipage documents including text and graphics using computer page layout tools

P8   Develop audiotapes that combine sounds and voice data from a variety of sources

P9   Produce videotapes that are organized, coherent, and well edited

P10   Create a personal database requiring the collection of data over time

Disseminate:

D1   Present relatively complex *Logo* or *HyperCard* (or similar) product including still pictures; flip card, path-based, and cell-based animations; sounds; graphics; and motion pictures

D2   Publish multipage printed documents including text and graphics

D3   Broadcast edited audiotape of moderate complexity

D4   Broadcast edited videotape of moderate complexity

D5   Broadcast video presentation over schoolwide Channel 1 (Whittle), citywide public Channel 28, or citywide ITFS schools-only equipment

D6   Advertise events, services, or products

D7   Display information and designs on various formats available

D8   Broadcast on closed circuit or cable television

D9   Broadcast filmed and live performances on television

D10   Distribute over available sources in Internet

How students should be able to use technology by the end of Grade 12

Access:

A1	Access and use complex electronic databases and communication networks of all types including, but not limited to, Internet
A2	Research using sensors, probes, and other specialized scientific tools as appropriate
A3	Gather information from spreadsheet, databasing software, and statistical packages, including the use of formulas and charting routines
A4	Search technologies for data and primary sources (publications and persons)
A5	Identify local, regional, and national databases and procedures for needed data
A6	Review online bulletin boards, databases, and electronic retrieval services for data

Produce:

P1	Create with complex computer painting and drawing tools and programs
P2	Create 3-D graphics using drawing and modeling tools
P3	Create changing images using computer digital-morphing programs
P4	Illustrate concrete and abstract concepts using computer-aided design and mathematical modeling
P5	Create CD-ROM simulations
P6	Create complex cell-based animations, including 3-D objects, using the computer
P7	Create complex *Logo* or *HyperCard* (or similar) programs including pictures; photographs; flip card, path-based, and cell-based animations; sounds; 3-D graphics; and motion pictures
P8	Develop multipage documents with information from a variety of sources, including text and graphics using appropriate computer page layout tools
P9	Create documents using a variety of fonts and type faces
P10	Assemble findings based on spreadsheets, databasing software, and statistical packages involving the use of formulas as appropriate
P11	Design graphic and text titles for digital video productions
P12	Develop digitally edited materials including audio, motion pictures, still-frame pictures, motion graphics, and still-frame graphics
P13	Design and develop a personal database of moderate complexity
P14	Illustrate concrete and abstract mathematical and scientific concepts
P15	Assemble information by creating, searching, and sorting databases
P16	Design and develop a dissemination design for video using ITFS microwave and satellite up-and-down links

Disseminate:

D1	Transmit complex *Logo* or *HyperCard* (or similar) computer product including pictures; photographs; flip card, path-based, and cell-based animations; sounds; 3-D graphics; and motion pictures
D2	Publish multipage printed documents, appropriately laid out, including text and graphics
D3	Transmit complex spreadsheet or database findings
D4	Telecast digital video product of some complexity

D5 Present computer-based animation program (cell- or path-based animations, or both)

D6 Publish reports generated from database searches

D7 Publish scientific investigations and results or recommendations

D8 Transmit a video presentation to secondary students using ITFS microwave, Whittle Channel 1 equipment, public Channel 28, cable hookups, and satellite up-and-down links to local schools or students in other school systems

D9 Share product or presentation with a panel of experts

Technology Connections
Fine Arts—Art: Grade 3

ART—STRUCTURE AND FUNCTION
CORRESPONDING PERFORMANCE BENCHMARK, PAGE 16

KEY ORGANIZING QUESTION:
What are different forms of art?

ACCESS	PRODUCE	DISSEMINATE
PERFORMANCE TASK I: You are going to teach a group of first graders about different types of art forms. You can include photographs, paintings, sketches, and sculptures. You may use pictures or you may take digital photographs of actual art examples.	**PERFORMANCE TASK I:** Copy your examples in correct sequence into a paint or draw program, a word processing program, or *HyperCard*. Create a composite sheet that contains all of the examples of common art forms grouped together in a common line. Make two copies for each student who will be working with you.	**PERFORMANCE TASK I:** Give each student two copies of the composite sheet that shows the examples of various art forms. Explain to them the differences in the art forms. Have them cut the first composite sheet apart and mix up the examples. Then have them group the tiny pictures into correct categories. They could check their work against their second composite.
PERFORMANCE TASK II: Your job is to create a display for the bulletin board in the main hall of your school. This bulletin board will be a visual representation of different art forms (e.g., photographs, drawings, sculptures, etc.). You must collect eight large color pictures of these different art forms.	**PERFORMANCE TASK II:** Create your pictures by using a digital camera. Take pictures of actual art or of pictures of art. Make sure you include different art forms. Download your pictures into the computer. Size your pictures and print them on the color printer. Frame your prints of different art forms. Using an appropriate computer program like *Print Shop* create a title banner for your bulletin board and also create labels for your various art forms.	**PERFORMANCE TASK II:** Arrange your framed prints on the bulletin board in the main hall. Make sure you include a title for your display. You should also include the printed labels for the various art forms. Invite a group of friends from another class to view your bulletin board. Explain to them how you created your materials and what you hope they will learn from the display.

Technology Connections
Fine Arts—Art: Grade 5

ART IN SOCIETY
CORRESPONDING PERFORMANCE BENCHMARK, PAGE 22

KEY ORGANIZING QUESTION:

What is the artist's role in the community?

ACCESS	PRODUCE	DISSEMINATE
PERFORMANCE TASK I: You are an artist and must design an object, a label, a cover, or a package that will make a contribution to the community. Take time to review such items as greeting cards, postage stamps, soup can labels, or CD covers to get ideas for your own design.	**PERFORMANCE TASK I:** Analyze the various approaches artists have taken with the products you reviewed. Decide what your product will be. Use the computer with a paint and draw program to create your product.	**PERFORMANCE TASK I:** Print your creation on a color printer and use it as you explain to a learning partner how this piece of art can make a contribution to the community.
PERFORMANCE TASK II: You are an artist and you must design a poster for the local arts and crafts show that will be held in your neighborhood. Review several poster examples and identify all of the important information that must be included in your poster.	**PERFORMANCE TASK II:** Create your poster using the computer and a program of your choice or one such as *Print Master Platinum*. Print your poster on a color printer and enlarge it using the color copy machine.	**PERFORMANCE TASK II:** Present your poster to the chairperson of the local arts and crafts show. Explain your ideas to this person and offer it as a community service for use in their advertising campaign.

**Technology Connections
Fine Arts—Art: Grade 12**

ART IN SOCIETY
CORRESPONDING PERFORMANCE BENCHMARK, PAGE 24

KEY ORGANIZING QUESTION:

What is the role of censorship or propaganda in art?

ACCESS	PRODUCE	DISSEMINATE
PERFORMANCE TASK I: You are a reporter investigating the topic of censorship or propaganda in art. Clearly identify your question and then proceed to identify a piece of art that is considered controversial. Your task is to gather personal reactions and responses to this art through a Web site.	**PERFORMANCE TASK I:** Capture a digital photograph of this artwork or scan a picture of it so you can use it on the Web site that you design and develop for this task. Be sure to design the page so you can solicit the information about personal reactions to this controversial piece of art. Analyze your collected data and organize it for an audiovisual presentation using a program like *Power Point*.	**PERFORMANCE TASK I:** Rehearse your audiovisual presentation and invite a group of your instructors and friends to view it. Ask them for their reactions and ideas following your presentation.
PERFORMANCE TASK II: You are a writer for a modern art museum and must write an article for one of their publications about a new piece of modern art that will be coming to the museum. For this task, select a piece of modern art that deals with a current controversial social issue. If you prefer, you may create your own piece of modern art for this project.	**PERFORMANCE TASK II:** Compare and contrast the various attitudes the public might display toward this piece of art. Organize your ideas into a logical sequence and write your article for the museum publication. Publish your article using a desktop publishing program and be sure to include several pictures of the art.	**PERFORMANCE TASK II:** Print out hard copies of your article and be prepared to present it to a group of art patrons. You may also want to distribute your article on the Internet through appropriate sites and gain reactions from a variety of viewers.

Technology Connections
Fine Arts—Art: Grade 8

ART IN WORLD CULTURES
CORRESPONDING PERFORMANCE BENCHMARK, PAGE 29

KEY ORGANIZING QUESTION:

What is the significance of past cultural contributions to society today?

ACCESS	PRODUCE	DISSEMINATE
PERFORMANCE TASK I: As a historian, you are to research and gather information on major contributions to society today from two different cultures of the past. Analyze your findings and then develop a technological scrapbook that depicts your identified examples. You may search CD-ROMs and /or encyclopedia programs or *Middle School Advantage* to identify items for use.	**PERFORMANCE TASK I:** Organize your ideas and transfer your identified items into a program like *Ultimate Scrap Book Creator*. Design and develop your scrapbook depicting the major contributions from two different cultures.	**PERFORMANCE TASK I:** Present your scrapbook as a computer project and print hard copies to accompany your presentation on the major contributions from two different cultures. Do your presentation for another class interested in this topic.
PERFORMANCE TASK II: As a historian, research and gather information on three to five useful objects from at least two different past cultures. Analyze your options and make your selections. You may use CD-ROMs, encyclopedia programs, or historical programs to locate your items.	**PERFORMANCE TASK II:** Use a digital camera to record the pictures of your selected objects or create a computer file for storage. Apply your selected items to a program like *Power Point* to create an audiovisual presentation.	**PERFORMANCE TASK II:** Present your audiovisual program to another class in your school or arrange to present it to a local fifth-grade class. Be sure to include published handouts to accompany your presentation.

Technology Connections
Fine Arts—Music: Grade 8

LISTENING
CORRESPONDING PERFORMANCE BENCHMARK, PAGE 61

KEY ORGANIZING QUESTION:

What effect does background music have on listeners/viewers?

ACCESS	PRODUCE	DISSEMINATE
PERFORMANCE TASK I: You are going to investigate the use of music in movies in setting a mood. Select a variety of movie types (drama, comedy, love story, etc.). View portions of the film and listen carefully to how the music is used.	**PERFORMANCE TASK I:** Select several strong examples from the movies you viewed and write a script for your own documentary video on the power of music in setting moods. Review your script and your ideas with a friend and make adjustments as needed. Create your video. Use music in the background for your introduction and credits so you can set a mood. Be sure to check the copyrights before you include the taped segments from your movies.	**PERFORMANCE TASK I:** Present your video to a drama class and lead a discussion with them on the power of music in setting moods for a scene. Ask them what the music conveys to them. Does it help or does it get in the way of their personal enjoyment?
PERFORMANCE TASK II: As a music director for consumers, take a trip through several shopping malls in your area and listen to the kinds of music different stores play over their PA systems. Select one store and talk to the manager. Explain that you are studying the effect music has on shoppers and that you are going to develop a tape for his store. Ask if he will play it and give you feedback on the reaction from shoppers.	**PERFORMANCE TASK II:** Analyze the conditions in the store of your choice, the merchandise they sell, and the type of customers they attract. Design and develop your audiotape and play it for your own test market or group of typical customers. Get their reactions. Make adjustments to the tape as you need.	**PERFORMANCE TASK II:** Present your tape to the store manager. You might want to survey a few customers to gain their reactions to your tape. Certainly you want the reactions of the store manager. Were you successful in affecting the sales? Was it positive or negative?

Technology Connections
Fine Arts—Music: Grade 12

MUSIC IN RELATION TO ART
CORRESPONDING PERFORMANCE BENCHMARK, PAGE 80

KEY ORGANIZING QUESTION:

How do artists use their skills and knowledge to influence societal change?

ACCESS	PRODUCE	DISSEMINATE
PERFORMANCE TASK I: As a community advocate, select a community health or safety issue that is important to you. Research the issue thoroughly and determine what type of 3-second community service message needs to be projected to the citizens.	**PERFORMANCE TASK I:** Clearly define your criteria for a quality public service announcement. Design and develop a script addressing your selected community issue. What must people do? What kind of public reaction will result in a safer population? Create a 3-minute public service announcement using a camcorder and/or digital camera. Review your results and make necessary changes.	**PERFORMANCE TASK I:** Meet with and present your public service announcement to the station or program manager at your local cable station. You may also want to enter your public service announcement in the statewide competition for such products. You might end up a national winner.
PERFORMANCE TASK II: As a historical investigator, collect examples of current and historical cartoons related to a specific theme, topic, or issue. Be sure to use the Internet as a valuable resource. Try to relate your research to a topic that causes strong feeling within you.	**PERFORMANCE TASK II:** Analyze your findings and determine how the creators used their artistic talents to influence society. Analyze the types of symbols and images the cartoonist used to influence the point of view or opinions of the viewers. For example, animals such as skunks have been used a lot to portray crooked politicians. Use a computer morphing program *(Print Artist Pro Morph)* as part of a multimedia presentation including specially selected music to communicate a personal position on a selected social issue.	**PERFORMANCE TASK II:** Present your program to a government or sociology class. Ask them to respond to your program (the visuals and the music) and to your intended message on a response sheet that you have designed and printed for them. Analyze their responses to determine how history might be documented or altered based on a combination of fact, bias, emotions, and point of view.

Technology Connections
Fine Arts—Music: Grade 3

MUSIC IN RELATION TO HISTORY/WORLD CULTURES
CORRESPONDING PERFORMANCE BENCHMARK, PAGE 83

KEY ORGANIZING QUESTION:
How does music from different cultures vary and how is it the same?

ACCESS	PRODUCE	DISSEMINATE
PERFORMANCE TASK I: As a historical researcher, select a specific country and gather as much historical information on that country as you can. Listen to music from your selected country. View videos if possible.	**PERFORMANCE TASK I:** Summarize the important ideas you would like others to know about your country and its music. Select key pictures and information to use in a multimedia computer presentation. Use a scanner to import pictures or transfer them from an encyclopedia disk. Create any charts that would be necessary for your program to convey necessary information. Include samples of the music as well.	**PERFORMANCE TASK I:** Present your multimedia presentation to a group of students from another class by using your computer with a Smart-Board, which is like a giant computer or projection device.
PERFORMANCE TASK II: As a researcher, select a country and gather as much historical information on that country as you can. Listen to various pieces of music that represent your country.	**PERFORMANCE TASK II:** Summarize the key ideas you would like to present to others. Select the key pictures to convey your ideas. You may use art if it is helpful. Use a color copier to create colored transparencies of your pictures. Select music from your country to go with each picture you plan to use. Create an audio tape. Create a script on a word processor.	**PERFORMANCE TASK II:** Use an overhead projector and a tape recorder to share your presentation with a group of students from another room. Ask them what they learned about your country from your presentation. Ask them how the music helped them understand the pictures.

Technology Connections
Fine Arts—Music: Grade 5

**Performance
Benchmark**

MUSIC IN RELATION TO HISTORY/WORLD CULTURES
CORRESPONDING PERFORMANCE BENCHMARK, PAGE 84

KEY ORGANIZING QUESTION:

How is war reflected in music?

ACCESS	PRODUCE	DISSEMINATE
PERFORMANCE TASK I: You are responsible for developing an assembly for your school on music from war time. Investigate several wars and identify pictures or pieces of art to represent them. Listen to music that was produced during those same time periods.	**PERFORMANCE TASK I:** Analyze the information you have identified and select pictures and music that will provide a strong composite of war music for your audience. Create a computer-generated multimedia presentation using the pictures, the music, and any captions you believe are necessary to convey your messages.	**PERFORMANCE TASK I:** Project your presentation onto a large screen for the assembly. Following the assembly, contribute your program to the school library or media center as a resource for classes to use in the future.
PERFORMANCE TASK II: In preparation for a Veterans' Day program for the senior citizens complex in your community, you are to research music that reflects the U.S. culture during World War II. Gather pictures from that era that represent the time. Listen to a variety of music from that time period.	**PERFORMANCE TASK II:** Analyze your gathered information and create a slide presentation using a digital camera. Be sure to capture selected portions of various musical pieces to accompany each slide. As a finale to your planned program, several teams of boys and girls could learn to how to swing dance or jitterbug to the music from that time. Design, write, and print out a program to accompany your presentation.	**PERFORMANCE TASK II:** Arrange for a time to present your program to the senior citizens complex or a meeting of American veterans. Ask them for their reactions to your program. How did your program make them feel?

4
PERFORMANCE DESIGNERS

The ultimate key to success with performance-based education is the creativity, rigor, and consistency of focus that must characterize the ongoing instructional process in the classroom. Student success with the performance benchmarks identified in this text depends on daily interactions with the learning actions. Students must feel empowered to demonstrate the learning actions being taught so they can internalize them, take ownership, and apply them easily in the benchmark performances. They must be able to do this through a continuous improvement process with a focus on quality criteria.

In order to accomplish the performance benchmarks in this text, learners must have daily practice with the routine of learning and demonstrating through learning actions as they gain new understanding about concepts from the different disciplines. They must recognize that only through continuous improvement will they achieve the defined quality that must be their goal.

If this is to occur, teachers must design lessons specifically addressing the learning actions (access, interpret, produce, disseminate, and evaluate). Instruction on these learning actions will engage students in gathering and interpreting information so they can produce a product, service, or performance with their newly acquired insights and knowledge. Then they can disseminate or give their product, service, or performance to an authentic audience. They do all of these learning actions with a continuous focus on evaluating themselves and their work against the identified quality criteria that the teacher will be looking for.

The performance designer is a tool for teachers to use when planning for students to engage in a significant demonstration that is an interactive experience for students designed to include essential content, competence (learning actions), context (issue, situation, and audience), and quality criteria.

The completed performance designer will describe the total performance or demonstration of significance. All of the students' actions will be clearly stated. The teacher uses this performance designer to develop the necessary instructional sequences that will support the attainment of each of the desired actions. Once students know how to do the actions, they are ready to pursue the planned performance.

The following organizer provides an overview. Each major section in the planner is identified and corresponds to a detailed explanation that follows.

PERFORMANCE DESIGNER FORMAT

I	**Ⓐ PURPOSE**...............................	What complex thinking process is the focus?	
	Ⓑ KEY ORGANIZING QUESTION..........	An issue or challenge to investigate.	
	Ⓒ ROLE.....................................	You are _____ who is expected to ...	

	(Do what?)	*(With what?)*	*(How well?)*
II	**Ⓓ** Access and **Ⓔ** interpret by...	**Ⓕ** CONTENT/CONCEPTS	**Ⓖ** QUALITY CRITERIA "Look fors"
III	*(In order to...* **Ⓗ** Produce by...	*...do what?)* **Ⓘ** PRODUCT/ PERFORMANCE	*(How well?)* **Ⓙ** QUALITY CRITERIA "Look fors"
IV	**Ⓚ** Disseminate by...	*(To/for whom? Where?)* **Ⓛ** AUDIENCE/ SETTING	*(How well?)* **Ⓜ** QUALITY CRITERIA "Look fors"

Section I

The first section of the designer serves as an organizer for the key elements that follow.

PERFORMANCE DESIGNER ELEMENT	REFLECTIVE QUESTIONS
Ⓐ PURPOSE The reason the performance is worth doing. This section may be tied to state- or district-level assessment. It will more often relate to a complex thinking process that is the result of applied critical-reasoning skills. (Example: drawing a conclusion, making a recommendation)	What do I want to be sure students are more competent doing when this performance is complete? Do I want them to be able to develop a range of possible solutions to a problem? Will they investigate an issue from outside school, form an opinion, or describe and support a point of view? What complex thinking skill is the core purpose of this performance?
Ⓑ KEY ORGANIZING QUESTION As with the purpose, the question focuses and organizes the entire performance. It combines with the role and the audience to define the context.	What will the students be accessing information about? Do I want to select the issue or question to be accessed, or will the students determine the learning they will pursue? Is the question or issue developmentally appropriate, and can I facilitate obtaining the resources that students will need for the issue? Do the students have any experiential background for this issue? Will the experience be limited to learning from the experiences of others?
Ⓒ ROLE When students take on a role, the point of view of the role adds a dimension not common to most learning. The role introduces the prompt that initiates the entire performance.	Will this role be authentic? Or is it a role-play? For example, students as artists, authors, and investigators are real roles for students. Students as lawyers, policemen, or city council members do not have the same level of authenticity. They would be role-playing, which is pretending to be someone. Will there be more than one role, or will students all be in the same role? How will I ensure that students will have a focused point of view to explore? In life outside school, who would answer this question or be concerned with this issue? What would that expert do? Who is the expert? What's the real role?

Section II

The second section of the performance designer focuses on having students carry out the learning actions of accessing and interpreting necessary content and concepts. The right-hand column of the top section defines the quality criteria, or "look fors," that will be taught, practiced, and assessed. These are the quality criteria of the performance benchmarks.

PERFORMANCE DESIGNER ELEMENT	REFLECTIVE QUESTIONS
D ACCESS AND Accessing actions might require students to interview, locate, or read for information. The importance of student involvement in acquiring information requires a shift from teacher as information provider to teacher as facilitator for information accessing.	Where can information be accessed? Are there experts who can be interviewed? What publications will be helpful? Which texts contain related information? Who can we contact on the Internet? What other resources are available?
E INTERPRET BY... *(Do what?)* Interpreting actions requires students to review what they have collected and decide what it means now that they have it. Students may categorize the information they have, compare it with what they already know, and process it in a variety of critical and creative ways.	How will students interact with the information they have collected? Will they formulate new questions? Will they begin to be asked to draw conclusions or perhaps make predictions at this point in the performance? Who will students interact with to communicate their initial interpretations of the information? Will they have a peer conference? Will I ask questions or give answers?
F CONTENT/CONCEPTS *(With what?)* This specifies the knowledge or information the students are to learn. The result at the end is only going to be as good as the information the students collect. The resources should go far beyond the text. The teacher should support with additional resources and literature examples.	What do the students need to know? Where will the information come from? What will be significant learning to retain after the performance is over? Why is it important for students to learn this? Where might they need to use it later? Next year? After they leave school? What connections can they make to other knowledge structures? What are different points of view?
G QUALITY CRITERIA *("Look fors")* *(How well?)* Quality criteria are the specifications for the performance. It is critical that these "look fors" be observable and measurable and that they represent high-quality performances. The quality criteria stated in the third column will integrate the learning actions in the left-hand column with the content/concept to be learned in the center column.	What would an expert interviewer or artist do? What would be observable in the performance of a quality questioner or researcher? How would I know one if I saw one? Do the criteria match the learning action that has been selected, and do they describe a logical and relevant application of the content/concept that is to be learned?

Section III

The third main section on the performance designer is organized similarly but focuses on the producing action or competence in the Learning Actions Wheel. The middle column of this section allows the teacher to describe or specify the nature of the product or performance the students are to generate. The right-hand column describes the quality criteria, or "look fors," that pertain to that product or production.

PERFORMANCE DESIGNER ELEMENT	REFLECTIVE QUESTIONS
Ⓗ PRODUCE BY... *(In order to...* Producing actions ask students to synthesize their learning, to bring what has been learned together into a cohesive whole that has relevance. Students might design, build, develop, create, construct, or illustrate.	How will students bring what they have learned together? What actions will lead to a product and keep the students in the role? Are there stages to the producing action, such as design and develop or draft and write? What are the essential actions that will lead to a product?
Ⓘ PRODUCT/PERFORMANCE *...do what?)* This describes the product, service, or production that the student will address. It should be something that will benefit the authentic audience.	What would an expert create? How does this product relate to the required or identified knowledge base? How does this product incorporate the required skills? What impact should the product have on the audience?
Ⓙ QUALITY CRITERIA ("Look fors") *(How well?)* Quality criteria describe the learning actions as they occur in conjunction with the development of the product, service, or production. It is critical that the criteria be observable, and measurable, and that it represent quality.	What would an excellent product look like? How could it be described? Will the product or production indicate the designing and developing that were used? How can it be precisely described in relationship to the learning actions? What are the essential actions the student will perform that relate to the producing verbs?

Section IV

The last section of the performance designer relates to the disseminating learning actions. It describes the sharing of the product. The middle column of this section clearly denotes the *audience* and the *setting*, or *context*, in which the performance will occur. These factors are critical in determining the realistic impact of the student's learning. The right-hand column will describe the quality criteria for this portion of the performance designer by combining the disseminating action in relationship with the authentic audience. It defines the purpose for the learning.

PERFORMANCE DESIGNER ELEMENT	REFLECTIVE QUESTIONS
Ⓚ DISSEMINATE BY... Learning actions at this stage of the role performance or demonstration have the learners presenting their products, services, or productions. The form of the presentation will vary depending on the original purpose. The learner might disseminate by explaining, teaching, or dancing.	What will be the most efficient and effective form of communicating this new product? Will students choose to broadcast or publish or teach? How does this form best relate to the product and the purpose? How does this delivery relate to the role?
Ⓛ AUDIENCE/SETTING *(To/for whom? Where?)* The audience is the recipient of the learners' product or production. The degree of authenticity will be reflected in the composition of the audience. The setting for this performance could be related to the original issue being investigated as well as the purpose for this investigation, or the natural location of the recipient.	Who will benefit from the students' learning? Who can use this recommendation or this finding? Is it another learner? Someone at another grade level? Is it a team of engineers at General Motors? Or young patients in a dentist's office? Where is the audience?
Ⓜ QUALITY CRITERIA **("Look fors")** *(How well?)* The criteria describe the specification for delivering the product, service, or performance. They are observable and represent quality.	What does a quality presentation look like? What are the essential elements that clearly define a quality presentation? How do the criteria connect the disseminating actions with the learner and the audience?

The performance designer gives teachers a very useful tool for continuously defining learning in terms of a realistic role that students must either individually or collectively take on and accomplish. The performance designer also continuously engages students in the range of learning actions that successful people engage in after they graduate from school, but it does so in the safe environment of school under the careful guidance of the teacher. Learners will demonstrate each role performance according to their developmental level of growth. Continuous involvement and experience with learning actions and quality criteria will result in demonstrated student improvement and continuous upleveling of quality criteria that will fully prepare students for any performance benchmark they are asked to demonstrate.

EXAMPLES OF LEARNING ACTIONS

ACCESS:
Investigate
Gather
Interview
Research
Listen
Observe
Collect
Search
Inquire
Survey
View
Discover
Read
Explore
Examine

INTERPRET:
Analyze
Explain
Paraphrase
Rephrase
Clarify
Compare
Contrast
Summarize
Integrate
Evaluate
Translate
Prioritize
Synthesize
Sort
Classify

PRODUCE:
Create
Design
Develop
Draw
Write
Lay out
Build
Draft
Invent
Erect
Sketch
Assemble
Compose
Illustrate
Generate

DISSEMINATE:
Publish
Perform
Teach
Present
Transmit
Display
Explain
Broadcast
Act
Advertise
Discuss
Send
Sing
Dance
Telecast

EVALUATE:
Review
Reflect
Assess
Revisit
Compare
Conclude
Generalize
Prove
Question
Refute
Support
Verify
Test
Realign
Judge

SAMPLE PERFORMANCE DESIGNER FOR GRADE 3

PURPOSE:
To analyze and make connections

FINE ARTS:
CRITIQUING ART
(SEE PAGE 37)

KEY ORGANIZING QUESTION:
How do you read a painting?

ROLE: *(You are ...)*
A shopper

(Who is expected to ...)

COMPETENCE (Do what?)	CONTENT/CONCEPTS (With what?)	QUALITY CRITERIA ("Look fors")
Access and interpret by ... observing	various copies of famous paintings	• Identify your purpose. • Note and identify details.
and summarizing	the way they make you feel and what you like about each painting.	• Summarize the important points. • Share your personal reactions.

COMPETENCE (In order to ...	PRODUCT/PERFORMANCE ... do what?)	QUALITY CRITERIA ("Look fors")
Produce by ... developing	a copy (a sketch, a drawing, or a painting) of the one of the famous paintings you would like to buy and hang in your room.	• Review possibilities. • Identify a delivery system. • Arrange and include all necessary details. • Create your painting.

COMPETENCE	AUDIENCE / SETTING (To/for whom? Where?)	QUALITY CRITERIA ("Look fors")
Disseminate by ... sharing and explaining	your copy with a group of friends and telling then how the original made you feel.	• Organize your ideas. • Include important information. • Provide details. • Ask for comments or suggestions.

SAMPLE PERFORMANCE DESIGNER FOR GRADE 5

PURPOSE:
To communicate a message

**FINE ARTS:
CREATING ART
(SEE PAGE 44)**

- -

KEY ORGANIZING QUESTION:
How can you use principles of art to communicate concepts from science or social studies?

- -

ROLE: *(You are ...)*
An illustrator

(Who is expected to ...)

COMPETENCE *(Do what?)*	CONTENT/CONCEPTS *(With what?)*	QUALITY CRITERIA *("Look fors")*
Access and interpret by ... gathering	information on a selected social studies or science topic or concept	• Identify your task. • Decide where to get materials and information. • Collect information from a variety of resources.
and prioritizing	the key ideas on this topic or concept.	• Identify the major points. • Select the most important.

COMPETENCE *(In order to ...*	PRODUCT/PERFORMANCE *... do what?)*	QUALITY CRITERIA *("Look fors")*
Produce by ... sketching and illustrating	a rough draft and a finished drawing of your topic that conveys key ideas and/or a special message.	• Organize the ideas into a first layout. • Include accurate representation. • Create a draft/sketch. • Check for impact and accuracy. • Create a finished product.

COMPETENCE	AUDIENCE / SETTING *(To/for whom? Where?)*	QUALITY CRITERIA *("Look fors")*
Disseminate by ... presenting and displaying	your drawing at the PTA meeting in the school library.	• Organize your ideas and your message. • Include important details. • Share your conclusions on communication through art. • Assemble the layout of your display.

SAMPLE PERFORMANCE DESIGNER FOR GRADE 8

PURPOSE:
Compare and contrast to draw a conclusion

FINE ARTS:
ART—STRUCTURE AND FUNCTION
(SEE PAGE 18)

- -

KEY ORGANIZING QUESTION:
How do you respond to various artistic styles?

- -

ROLE: *(You are ...)*
A museum tour guide

(Who is expected to ...)

COMPETENCE *(Do what?)*	CONTENT/CONCEPTS *(With what?)*	QUALITY CRITERIA *("Look fors")*
Access and interpret by ... investigating and analyzing	at least five pieces of art that represent different styles of art the unique characteristics of each of these pieces and determine how they make you feel.	• Identify your purpose. • Clearly state the unique features you notice. • Provide detailed descriptions. • Select the most important aspects to compare. • Identify the unique reactions that result.

COMPETENCE *(In order to ...*	PRODUCT/PERFORMANCE *... do what?)*	QUALITY CRITERIA *("Look fors")*
Produce by ... designing and developing	a written description of each piece of art that includes unique characteristics about the style and also descriptions of your personal reactions.	• Identify your audience. • Organize your information. • Create a draft. • Check for impact and accuracy. • Create a finished draft.

COMPETENCE	AUDIENCE / SETTING *(To/for whom? Where?)*	QUALITY CRITERIA *("Look fors")*
Disseminate by ... presenting and explaining	these selected pieces of art to a group of students from the fourth grade.	• Select appropriate method and materials for presenting. • Organize your ideas and your message. • Include important details. • Share your personal reactions.

SAMPLE PERFORMANCE DESIGNER FOR GRADE 12

PURPOSE:
To create a design/model

FINE ARTS:
PHILOSOPHY OF ART
(SEE PAGE 51)

- -

KEY ORGANIZING QUESTION:
What is the nature and meaning of art?

- -

ROLE: *(You are ...)*
An artist

(Who is expected to ...)

COMPETENCE (Do what?)	CONTENT/CONCEPTS (With what?)	QUALITY CRITERIA ("Look fors")
Access and interpret by ... researching	the moods, attitudes, trends, values, and beliefs of a sample of citizens in your community about the future	• Identify your purpose. • Design a survey instrument. • Collect responses from a representative sampling of citizens.
and translating	your findings into a composite of the community's beliefs and values.	• Summarize the main ideas. • Interpret your finding through a sculpture design.

COMPETENCE (In order to ...	PRODUCT/PERFORMANCE ... do what?)	QUALITY CRITERIA ("Look fors")
Produce by ... drafting and designing	a sculpture that will be the centerpiece of a new fountain in the park by the library and the city hall.	• Create a preliminary sketch. • Include dimensions, materials, and several views. • Solicit reactions. • Adjust and redesign as necessary. • Create a final product.

COMPETENCE	AUDIENCE / SETTING (To/for whom? Where?)	QUALITY CRITERIA ("Look fors")
Disseminate by ... presenting and displaying	your final product with detailed information for construction to representatives from your city council.	• Identify and explain your purpose. • Organize your message and your materials. • Include necessary details. • Ask for reactions.

SAMPLE PERFORMANCE DESIGNER FOR GRADE 3

PURPOSE:
To make connections and create music

FINE ARTS:
CREATING
(SEE PAGE 65)

KEY ORGANIZING QUESTION:
What kinds of decisions do composers make?

ROLE: *(You are ...)*
A composer

(Who is expected to ...)

COMPETENCE (Do what?)	CONTENT/CONCEPTS (With what?)	QUALITY CRITERIA ("Look fors")
Access and interpret by ... exploring	various emotions and a variety of instrumental sounds	• Identify your purpose. • Select an emotion to convey. • Survey a variety of sounds.
and rephrasing	the selected sounds.	• Choose sounds that match your emotion.

COMPETENCE (In order to ...	PRODUCT/PERFORMANCE ... do what?)	QUALITY CRITERIA ("Look fors")
Produce by ... arranging	the selected sounds into a piece of music.	• Organize the sounds to project a melody. • Listen carefully to your sounds for the emotion you want to project.

COMPETENCE	AUDIENCE / SETTING (To/for whom? Where?)	QUALITY CRITERIA ("Look fors")
Disseminate by ... practicing	your composition with voice and instrumental sounds	• Rehearse your piece of music. • Use sounds appropriately.
and performing	it for another group in your class.	• Present before your selected audience. • Evaluate your audience's reaction.

SAMPLE PERFORMANCE DESIGNER FOR GRADE 5

PURPOSE:
To draw a conclusion

FINE ARTS:
MUSIC IN RELATION TO ART
(SEE PAGE 76)

KEY ORGANIZING QUESTION:
How can the arts be used to influence consumers?

ROLE: *(You are ...)*
A wise consumer

(Who is expected to ...)

COMPETENCE *(Do what?)*	CONTENT/CONCEPTS *(With what?)*	QUALITY CRITERIA *("Look fors")*

Access and interpret by ...
 	
   investigating
 	
   and examining and analyzing
	a product that many people use
	
	the advertising campaign used to market it.
		• Identify your purpose.
		• Survey a target group.
		• Select information according to options.
		• Prioritize your findings.

COMPETENCE *(In order to ...*	PRODUCT/PERFORMANCE *... do what?)*	QUALITY CRITERIA *("Look fors")*
Produce by ... designing and developing	a detailed script and plan for an advertising campaign that addresses an identified issue or product.	• Review the information. • Create a rough outline of your plan. • Edit for sequence and details. • Create your final draft.

COMPETENCE	AUDIENCE / SETTING *(To/for whom? Where?)*	QUALITY CRITERIA *("Look fors")*
Disseminate by ... presenting and explaining	your advertising campaign ideas to a group of visiting business people from the community.	• Identify purpose of campaign. • Develop a logical sequence. • Arrange details and materials. • Include relevant information. • Restate main ideas. • Close presentation and ask for feedback.

SAMPLE PERFORMANCE DESIGNER GRADE 8

PURPOSE:
To create a proposal or program

FINE ARTS:
MUSIC IN RELATION TO HISTORY/WORLD CULTURES
(SEE PAGE 85)

KEY ORGANIZING QUESTION:
How do you distinguish between music of the Baroque period and music if the Classical period?

ROLE: *(You are ...)*
A musical adviser

(Who is expected to ...)

COMPETENCE *(Do what?)*	CONTENT/CONCEPTS *(With what?)*	QUALITY CRITERIA *("Look fors")*
Access and interpret by ... researching and listening and evaluating	to many examples of Baroque and Classical music the differences between the two types of music.	• Identify your purpose. • Listen to many examples. • Identify the unique traits. • Identify the moods/feelings. • Document the information. • Categorize the differences.

COMPETENCE *(In order to ...*	PRODUCT/PERFORMANCE *... do what?)*	QUALITY CRITERIA *("Look fors")*
Produce by ... planning and creating	a musical program for a formal state dinner starting with the entrance of the guests, the meal, and the entertainment afterward.	• Identify a time period (how long the program will last). • Preview possibilities. • Identify a beginning. • Arrange details. • Create a final draft. • Review the arrangement.

COMPETENCE	AUDIENCE / SETTING *(To/for whom? Where?)*	QUALITY CRITERIA *("Look fors")*
Disseminate by ... presenting and distributing	your planned program (which should include an audiotape) to the program director of the local symphony orchestra or a representative.	• Arrange your meeting time. • Plan your opening approach. • Organize ideas and materials. • Communicate effectively. • Provide a copy of your tape and plan. • Elicit feedback.

SAMPLE PERFORMANCE DESIGNER FOR GRADE 12

PURPOSE:
To analyze and create a product

FINE ARTS:
MUSIC IN RELATION TO HISTORY/WORLD CULTURES
(SEE PAGE 86)

KEY ORGANIZING QUESTION:
How does music communicate distinct characteristics of time, place, or culture?

ROLE: *(You are ...)*
A musical producer

(Who is expected to ...)

COMPETENCE (Do what?)	CONTENT/CONCEPTS (With what?)	QUALITY CRITERIA ("Look fors")
Access and interpret by ... investigating and summarizing	a particular social, cultural, or economic theme from our history the significant aspects of the theme or events through selected art and musical pieces.	• Identify your purpose. • Utilize a variety of reliable resources. • Identify possibilities. • Match ideas with appropriate music. • Select the key ideas and music for your idea or theme.

COMPETENCE (In order to ...	PRODUCT/PERFORMANCE ... do what?)	QUALITY CRITERIA ("Look fors")
Produce by ... designing and developing	a video script that could be used to teach the important historical concepts you have identified.	• Identify your audience. • Select appropriate information. • Create a working outline. • Refine and extend to the fullest. • Adjust as needed. • Create a final script.

COMPETENCE	AUDIENCE / SETTING (To/for whom? Where?)	QUALITY CRITERIA ("Look fors")
Disseminate by ... taping and broadcasting	your script as a video it to other students or to the community over your local cable channel.	• Arrange all details and materials. • Produce the videotape. • Transmit to your audience.

APPENDIX: BLANK TEMPLATES

PERFORMANCE DESIGNER

PURPOSE:

- -

KEY ORGANIZING QUESTION:

- -

ROLE: *(You are ...)*

(Who is expected to ...)

COMPETENCE *(Do what?)*	CONTENT/CONCEPTS *(With what?)*	QUALITY CRITERIA *("Look fors")*
Access and interpret by ...		

COMPETENCE *(In order to ...)*	PRODUCT/PERFORMANCE *... do what?)*	QUALITY CRITERIA *("Look fors")*
Produce by ...		

COMPETENCE	AUDIENCE / SETTING *(To/for whom? Where?)*	QUALITY CRITERIA *("Look fors")*
Disseminate by ...		

Burz and Marshall. *Performance-Based Curriculum for Music and the Visual Arts: From Knowing to Showing.* © 1999 by Corwin Press, Inc.

Fine Arts:
Grade ___

CONTENT/CONCEPT STANDARD ___

KEY ORGANIZING QUESTION:

KEY COMPETENCES	KEY CONCEPTS AND CONTENT	PERFORMANCE TASKS
		PERFORMANCE TASK I:
		PERFORMANCE TASK II:

QUALITY CRITERIA:

Technology Connections
_____ : Grade ___

**Performance
Benchmark**

KEY ORGANIZING QUESTION:

ACCESS	PRODUCE	DISSEMINATE
PERFORMANCE TASK I:	**PERFORMANCE TASK I:**	**PERFORMANCE TASK I:**
PERFORMANCE TASK II:	**PERFORMANCE TASK II:**	**PERFORMANCE TASK II:**

BIBLIOGRAPHY

Anderson, W. M. (1991). *Teaching music with a multicultural approach.* Reston, VA: Music Educators National Conference.

Anderson, W. M., & Campbell, P. S. (1989). *Multicultural perspectives in music education.* Reston, VA: Music Educators National Conference.

Anderson, W. M., & Lawrence, J. E. (1985). *Integrating music into the classroom.* Belmont, CA: Wadsworth.

Beane, J. A. (Ed.). (1995). *Toward a coherent curriculum.* Alexandria, VA: Association for Supervision and Curriculum Development.

Bennett, R. (1980). *Form and design.* New York: Cambridge University Press.

Bennett, R. (1987). *History of music.* New York: Cambridge University Press.

Bennett, R. (1992). *Investigating musical styles.* New York: Cambridge University Press.

Bredekamp, S., (Ed.). (1987). *Developmentally appropriate practice in early childhood programs serving children from birth through age 8.* Washington, DC: National Association for the Education of Young Children.

Brittain, L. W. (1979). *Creativity, art, and the young child.* New York: Macmillan.

Carnegie Council on Adolescent Development. (1990, January). *Turning points: Preparing American youth for the 21st century.* New York: Carnegie Corp.

Chosky, L. (1988). *The Kodaly method: Comprehensive music education from infant to adult.* Englewood Cliffs, NJ: Prentice Hall.

Consortium of National Arts Education. (1994). *Dance, music, theatre, visual arts: What every young American should know and be able to do in the arts.* Reston, VA: Author.

Cripps, C. (1988). *Popular music in the 20th century.* New York: Cambridge University Press.

Dasher, R. T. (1975). *Music around the world.* Portland, ME: J. Weston Walch.

Edwards, B. (1979). *Drawing on the right side of the brain: A course in enhancing creativity and artistic confidence.* Los Angeles: J. P. Tarcher.

Fowler, C. (1988). *Sing!* Houston, TX: Hinshaw Music.

Fowler, C. (1994). *Music: Its role and importance in our lives.* Geneva, IL: Macmillan.

Frazee, J., with Kreuter, K. (1987). *Discovering Orff.* New York: Schott Music.

Goffin, S. G., & Tull, C. Q. (1984, January). Ideas! Creating problem-solving possibilities for young children. *Dimensions,* pp. 15-19.

Gridley, M. C. (1989). *Jazz styles (3rd ed.).* New York: Prentice Hall.

Hammond, S. (1994). *Classical kids, the classroom collection.* Toronto, Canada: The Children's Group.

Haritun, R. A. (1994), *Music teacher's survival guide.* West Hyack, NY: Parker.

High Success Network. (1986, Spring). Designing student role performances. *Outcomes: A Quarterly Journal of the Network for Outcomes-Based Schools, 5*(3), 2-9.

Howard, J. (1990). *Learning to compose.* New York: Cambridge University Press.

King, J. A., & Evans, K. M. (1991, October). Can we achieve outcome-based education? Integrating the curriculum. *Educational Leadership,* pp. 73-75.

Kuzmich, N. (1986). *Musical growth: A process of involvement.* Toronto, Canada: Gordon V. Thompson.

Lasky, L., & Mukerji, R. (1987). *Art basics for young children.* Washington, DC: National Association for the Education of Young Children.

Lowenfeld, V., & Brittain, L. (1987). *Creative and mental growth.* New York: Macmillan.

Machlis, J. (1992). *The enjoyment of music.* New York: Norton.

Menuhin, Y., & Davis, C. W. (1979). *The music of man.* Toronto, Canada: Methuen.

Minnesota Department of Education. (1991). *Model learner outcomes for art education.* St. Paul, MN: Author.

National Art Education Association. (1985). *The history of art education: Proceedings from the Penn State Conference.* College Park, PA: Author.

National Art Education Association. (1986). *Quality art education: Goals for schools.* Reston, VA: Author.

Pugh, A. (1991). *Women in music.* New York: Cambridge University Press.

Ragans, R. (1988). *Art talk.* Sacramento, CA: Glencoe.

Rao, D. (1994). *We will sing!* New York: Cambridge University Press.

Rasmussen, K. (1988, Spring). *Arts education: A cornerstone of basic education. Curriculum update* (pp. 1-7). Alexandria, VA: Association of Supervision and Curriculum Development.

Read, H. (1994). *Education through art.* New York: Cambridge University Press.

Sadie, S. (Ed.). (1984). *The new Grove dictionary of musical instruments.* London: Macmillan.

Spady, W. (1988, October). Organizing for results: the basis of authentic restructuring and reform. *Educational Leadership,* pp. 4-8.

Spady, W. G., & Marshall, K. J. (1991, October). Beyond traditional outcomes-based education. *Educational Leadership,* pp. 67-72.

South Carolina Department of Education. (1982). *Basic art skills.* Columbia, SC: Author.

Tillman, J. B. (1991). *Light the candles! (Songs of praise and ceremony from around the world).* New York: Cambridge Press.

U.S. Department of Education. (1994). *The vision for arts education in the 21st century.* Reston, VA: Author.

Wheeler, L., & Raebeck, L. (1972). *Orff and Kodaly adapted for the elementary school.* Dubuque, IA: Wm. C. Brown.

Wingell, R. (1983). *Experiencing music.* Sherman Oaks, CA: Alfred.

CORWIN
PRESS

The Corwin Press logo — a raven striding across an open book — represents the happy union of courage and learning. We are a professional-level publisher of books and journals for K–12 educators, and we are committed to creating and providing resources that embody these qualities. Corwin's motto is "Success for All Learners."